KERLY'S

LAW OF

TRADE MARKS

AND TRADE NAMES

TWELFTH EDITION

FIRST SUPPLEMENT

By

THE HON. SIR ROBIN JACOB

One of Her Majesty's Justices of the High Court

Master of the Bench of Gray's Inn

DAVID KITCHIN

One of Her Majesty's Counsel

JAMES MELLOR

Barrister

LONDON
SWEET & MAXWELL
1994

Twelfth Edition (1986) By T.A. Blanco White and Robin Jacob
First Supplement (1994) By Robin Jacob, David Kitchin and James Mellor

Published in 1994 by
Sweet and Maxwell Limited of
South Quay Plaza, 183 Marsh Wall,
London E14 9FT
Typeset by Mendip Communications Ltd.,
Frome, Somerset
Printed in Great Britain by
The Headway Press Ltd.

No natural forests were destroyed to make this product:
only farmed timber was used and re-planted

**A CIP catalogue record for this book is
available from the British Library**

ISBN Main Work 0 421 35060 1

Supplement 0 421 51040 4

PREFACE

United Kingdom registered trade mark law is about to start again. From scratch. The near 120-year-old regime begun by the Trade Marks Act 1876, itself founded upon earlier equitable principles, is being set aside by the need for common rules for trade marks in the Common Market. Some may say, "why bring *Kerly* up to date now – just when we do not need to know any of the soon-to-be discarded law?" There are many reasons. First, on a mundane level, the questioner's assumption of an immediate complete discard of the old would not be quite right. The new system will have transitional arrangements which matter for a few years. Second, a number of aspects of the old regime will carry over to the new – for instance procedural aspects of the conduct of oppositions in the Registry. Then again some matters (*e.g.* the evaluation of evidence, especially opinion polls) are likely to be the same for the new system. Moreover, the law of passing-off is not intended to be changed. More fundamentally, for those interested in the conceptual view of law, the old law will provide important insights into the inherent problems of trade mark law. Distinctiveness, what a trade mark is for, the relationship between a trade mark and goodwill, what a trade mark licence means, how much should rival traders be allowed to use each other's marks comparatively, what a trade mark licence really implies, and so on, are not matters which will go away. This will be so even if the new system provides a different answer or indeed the same answer for different reasons. Knowledge of how those questions were coped with before will enable those who deal with the new law to grapple better with it. Finally there are many users of *Kerly* abroad whose laws are based on the old system, and we hope an updating for them will be useful.

The last (12th) edition of *Kerly* was in 1986. There would have been a new edition earlier but we kept getting told there would be a new Act very shortly. So we waited: paralysed by rumour from year to year. Quite a lot has happened since the last edition, for instance a few cases of importance (*e.g.* "*Jif*"), the establishment and integration of service marks into the system besides an accretion of case law affecting a variety of minor aspects of law and practice. This Supplement is designed to bring the Twelfth Edition up to date to the end of 1993. Where it has been possible to include more recent material, we have done so. We hope that the Main Work plus the Supplement will provide a basis for the future, for both the United Kingdom and overseas.

Specifically, we have covered all cases reported to the end of the volumes of reports (both R.P.C. and F.S.R.) for 1993. We have included some later cases too, some reported and some not.

For those who do not know, it is perhaps worthwhile spelling out in more detail the imminent changes. The 1988 E.C. Trade Marks Directive (89/104) has been in force since January 1, 1993, but it appears to have had little effect in practice so far. The Bill currently in Parliament follows the wording of the Directive very closely. There will be some interesting questions of interpretation to be decided in due course. For a while, at least, trade mark law is likely to be less certain than it is now. Indeed in some areas the new law may introduce areas of permanent uncertainty, by setting factual questions which do not admit of a predictable answer. For instance the scope of goods covered by a registration is to include "similar goods" to those of the registration. This is likely to be a very fuzzy test.

The new Act is designed not only to implement the Directive but also to "effect a general modernisation of the law of trade marks" and to enable the United Kingdom to comply with the various international obligations. Thus, there will be provision for the Community Trade Mark, provision to enable effect to be given to the Protocol to the Madrid Agreement (effectively so that the U.K. can finally ratify the Agreement) and provisions to implement some trade mark obligations under the Paris Convention.

Even with a new Act in force, provisions of the 1938 Act will continue to apply in a number of important respects, at least for a while. Thus, issues as to how the Directive affects the 1938 Act will also continue to be live.

The scheme for the transitional provisions currently proposed is broadly as follows:

Applications for registration pending at the date of commencement of the new Act will continue to be dealt with under the old law, save that, in the case of applications that have not been advertised by commencement, the applicant may elect to have the registrability of the mark dealt with under the new Act.

Existing registrations will generally have effect as if registered under the new Act. As to infringement, the new Act will apply to acts committed after the date of commencement and the old law will apply to acts committed before the date of commencement. A saving provision will permit a person to continue after commencement any use which did not amount to infringement under the old law.

Applications for revocation for non-use or rectification which are pending at the date of commencement, will continue to be dealt with under the old law.

A new Act will result in a new edition of *Kerly*. It remains to be seen the extent to which case law, established under the 1938, and earlier, Acts will continue to be relevant. A new edition will also give us the opportunity to bring up to date those chapters not directly affected by the content of the new Act. In particular, we propose to reform the chapter on passing-off so that it not only reflects the more modern approach of the leading authorities, but is easier to use.

In the meantime, the final obstacles to the Regulation for the Community Trade Marks have been resolved. It was adopted on December 19, 1993. The CTM office is to be in Alicante. They will use five official languages –

English, French, German, Italian and Spanish. Whether there really is a significant demand for Community-wide trade marks not already met by the use of parallel national offices remains to be seen. A lot will depend upon cost. But even so it is common for traders to use different trade marks in different states simply for marketing reasons. The extreme form of such a reason are those cases (of which many readers will know good examples) where a mark perfectly good in one language has an unfortunate connotation in another. Trade marks are not like patents in this respect.

We have taken the deliberate decision to confine ourselves in this Supplement to matters as they stand under the 1938 Act. The new Act is not yet finalised and we have not made any analysis of its provisions (nor of the Community Trade Mark Regulations or Madrid Protocol) here. All of those matters will receive our full attention in the new edition of *Kerly*.

We conclude by pointing out that both the next edition will be and, indeed, this Supplement is, the first attempt at work on *Kerly* which has not involved Thomas Blanco White, Q.C., since he prepared the Ninth Edition in 1966. His work was of prominence, therefore, for over 25 years. We only hope that we can look after *Kerly* as well as he did. We miss his input but are glad to say that he remains fit and well – perhaps even better now that he has escaped from intellectual property.

R.J.   D.K., J.M.
Royal Courts of Justice   8 New Square, Lincoln's Inn

HOW TO USE THIS SUPPLEMENT

This First Supplement to the Twelfth Edition of Kerly's Law of Trade Marks and Trade Names is ordered according to the structure of the Main Work.

At the beginning of the Supplement, the Table of Contents from the Main Work has been included. Where a heading on this Table of Contents has been marked with a square pointer, then there is relevant material in the Supplement to which you should refer. The mini Table of Contents which precedes the Appendices in the Main Work has also been included in the Supplement, and it also denotes change to the original material in the manner outlined above.

Within each Chapter or Appendix updating information is referenced to the relevant paragraph in the Main Work.

CONTENTS

CONTENTS

APPENDICES

TABLE OF CASES

TABLE OF EUROPEAN CASES

TABLE OF STATUTES

Australia

Northern Ireland

TABLE OF RULES & ORDERS

RULES OF THE SUPREME COURT

TABLES OF TREATIES AND CONVENTIONS

EEC Treaty

Other International Treaties and Conventions

TABLE OF E.C. DIRECTIVES

THE 1988 TRADE MARKS DIRECTIVE

Introduction

1A–01

The E.C.'s 1988 Trade Marks Directive[1] is now, belatedly,[2] in the course of implementation by the United Kingdom Parliament. There is expected to be a Trade Marks Act 1994 in force, perhaps, by the end of 1994. The Directive is potentially of importance now and, despite the new Act, will be of importance after. Before the Act comes into force there may be cases where our previous existing law under the 1938 Act has been modified by aspects of the Directive which take effect now. Parties may say that the Directive gives them rights or defences now by reason of the United Kingdom's failure to implement the Directive. So even now questions of the extent, if any, of direct effect may arise. This in turn, of course, could involve questions of the proper interpretation of the Directive itself.

Once the new Act comes into force the Directive will continue to affect our law in a number of different ways. Primarily, it will be used as a guide to interpretation of portions of the new Act which purport to implement it, whether of the mandatory or optional provisions. So again there will be questions of the proper interpretation of the Directive. Moreover, if, as seems likely, the new Act in places differs in its wording from the Directive, there will be questions as to whether that is a difference of substance or of language only. In most cases it is likely that the courts will hold any difference to be only of language – after all the Act is supposed to be implementing the Directive. But there is the remote possibility that the language of our Act may be so different as to be incapable of being interpreted in accordance with the Directive. Were this to happen then arguments arising out of non-implementation of the mandatory parts of the Directive could arise even under the new Act.

Recent case law in other areas of E.C. law has generated a good deal of debate as to how the Directive may be relied upon here even before implementation. So far the debate has been largely academic, but may become important in a suitable case. Here we do no more than set out a summary of the available arguments – Direct Effect, Indirect Effect, and Damages for failure to implement. The arguments require a degree of knowledge of the principles and terminology of E.C. law.

---

[1] Council Directive 89/104: EEC [1989] O.J. L40/1, *post*, paras. A1A–1 *et seq.*
[2] The due date for implementation was January 1, 1993.

1A–02   E.C. Legislation

Article 189 of the Treaty of Rome provides that the Council and the Commission shall, in accordance with the provisions of the Treaty, make regulations, issue directives, take decisions, make recommendations or deliver opinions. For present purposes only regulations and directives need be considered. Article 189 goes on to specify that,

"a regulation shall have general application. It shall be binding in its entirety and directly applicable in all Member States."

"Directly applicable" means that nothing further need be done to make a Regulation part of the law of a Member State. In fact, by joining the E.C., each Member State has already agreed that regulations form part of its law and that they override any inconsistent national legislation. However:

"A directive shall be binding, as to the result to be achieved, upon each Member State to which it is addressed, but shall leave to the national authorities the choice of form and methods."

A directive is just that. It is a piece of legislation directed to Member States telling them to make national legislation in accordance with the directive. Unlike a regulation, a directive allows each Member State a certain amount of choice as to what it passes into law and how.

1A–03   The 1988 Trade Marks Directive

The Directive is set out in full in Appendix 1A, *post*. The result which the Directive is to achieve is the harmonisation of trade mark law throughout the Community. This does not mean a uniform Community law of trade marks, as is apparent from the fact that certain provisions in the Directive are mandatory and some optional.

Generally, the mandatory provisions say "shall", whereas the optional provisions say "may", although a notable exception is Article 2 which says what can be a "mark":

"A trade mark may consist of any sign capable of being represented graphically, particularly words, including personal names, designs, letters, numerals, the shape of goods or their packaging, provided that such signs are capable of distinguishing the goods or services of one undertaking from those of other undertakings."

The aim of harmonisation would be very significantly undermined if this was not interpreted as a list of signs which *must* be treated as being registrable marks provided they are capable of distinguishing. Thus Article 2 has to be interpreted as a mandatory provision.

It will be apparent that provisions in the Directive which are optional cannot be invoked unless or until the United Kingdom chooses to implement them. Thus, in advance of United Kingdom legislation in final form, the remainder of this discussion is limited to the mandatory provisions of the Directive.

Direct effect 1A–04

Although not stated in the Treaty, it is the settled law of the European Court of Justice that directives are capable of having direct effect.[3] The concept behind "direct effect" is that obligations imposed on Member States[4] can be construed so as to give rise to correlative rights in favour of and enforceable by individuals against the Member States concerned. Whether any particular provision has direct effect is determined according to a test comprising three elements:

(1) The provision must impose a clear and precise obligation on Member States.
(2) The provision must be unconditional, *i.e.* subject to no limitation. If, however, there is a limitation, its nature and extent must be clearly defined.
(3) The implementation of the provision must not require the adoption of any subsequent rules or regulations, whether on the part of any Community institution or Member State. In particular this means that Member States must not be left with a discretion as to how or whether to implement the provision in question.

Direct effect is of limited application since it only works vertically against the Member State and its organs and not horizontally against other companies or individuals. Therefore the most likely application of this principle is in the Registry in relation to an application for a "mark", such as the shape of a distinctive container, which falls outside the definitions in the 1938 Act. Clearly the scope of a "trade mark" under Article 2 is broader than the interpretation given to "mark" and "trade mark" under the 1938 Act.[5]

Indirect effect 1A–05

The so-called principle of "indirect effect" is in fact nothing more than a rule of interpretation. It stems from Article 5 of the Treaty which provides:

"Member States shall take all appropriate measures, whether general or particular, to ensure fulfilment of the obligations arising out of this Treaty or resulting from action taken by the institutions of the Community. They shall facilitate the achievement of the Community's tasks.

[3] Case 26/62 *Van Gend en Loos v. Nederlandse Belastringadministratie* [1963] E.C.R. 1; [1963] C.M.L.R. 105.
[4] The principle also applies in respect of community institutions and even individuals, but in the present context they can be ignored.
[5] See paras. 2–01 to 2–03 in the Main Work and the corresponding notes in this Supplement, *post.*

They shall abstain from any measure which could jeopardise the attainment of the objectives of this Treaty."

Case law of the European Court of Justice[6] has combined Article 189 (in relation to directives) with the general obligation contained in Article 5 to impose an obligation on the courts of Member States to interpret domestic legislation in the light of the text and objectives of an applicable directive – the words of a United Kingdom statute are to be construed, so far as is possible, as intended to carry out the Community obligation to which they give effect. This type of "soft" interpretation leaves the national legislation intact and is only required where there is a genuine question of interpretation before the court. It is a sensible approach when the national legislation was supposed to implement the directive in question.

1A–06   Recently the European Court of Justice appeared to extend the scope of this interpretative obligation. In *Marleasing*[7] the Court said it applied to national law whether adopted *before or after* the directive in question. This judgment has generated a good deal of academic debate as to how far the obligation now extends.

The application of *Marleasing* requires care, particularly where it is said that an English Act of Parliament passed in 1938 is to be interpreted in the light of a European Community Council Directive drafted 50 years later.

On the most extreme view it is argued that *Marleasing* imposes an obligation of "hard" interpretation, which is not really interpretation at all. Essentially, "hard" interpretation means that the provisions of a directive override national law. There are a number of very serious obstacles to this argument. First, this type of "hard" interpretation would promote directives almost to the same status as regulations, when they are clearly different. Second, in practice it would give directives direct effect not merely against the state (vertical) but also between individuals (horizontal), whereas in *Marleasing* itself the Court expressly confirmed that a directive could not of itself impose obligations on an individual.

Essentially, this extreme view is untenable. It is inconsistent with the judgment in the case itself and with previous[8] cases. Both the Court of Appeal and the House of Lords have already considered the effect of *Marleasing* in a different context.[9] Their approach was based very much on the words used in *Marleasing* (and apparently ignored by those who argue for "hard" interpretation) that,

---

[6] Case 14/83 *Von Colson and Kamann v. Land Nordrhein-Westfalen* [1984] E.C.R. 1891; [1986] 2 C.M.L.R. 430, and Case 79/83 *Harz v. Deutsche Tradex* [1984] E.C.R. 1921; [1986] 2 C.M.L.R. 430.

[7] Case C-106/89 *Marleasing SA v. La Comercial Internacional de Alimentacion SA* [1990] 1 E.C.R. 4135 [1992] 1 C.M.L.R. 305.

[8] *e.g.* Case 152/84 *Marshall v. Southampton and South-West Hampshire Area Health Authority* [1986] E.C.R. 723; [1986] 1 C.M.L.R. 688, expressly approved in *Marleasing*.

[9] *Webb v. EMO Air Cargo (U.K.) Ltd.* [1992] 2 All E.R. 43 (C.A.) and [1992] 4 All E.R. 929 (H.L.).

"in applying national law, whether the provisions in question were adopted before or after the directive, the national court called upon to interpret it is required to do so, so far as possible, in the light of the wording and the purpose of the directive in order to achieve the result pursued by the latter and comply with [Article 189(3)]"[10]

"so far as possible" indicating that it is not possible to distort the meaning of domestic law to fit with a directive.[11]

If properly interpreted, *Marleasing* may be capable of being deployed with effect in the right circumstances. The following are suggestions: **1A–07**

(a) There are provisions in the 1938 Act to which a judicial gloss has been applied. Now that the 1988 Directive is in force, it can be argued that it is no longer possible to apply the traditional judicial gloss, but that the court must interpret the words of the 1938 Act in the light of the applicable provisions in the Directive.
(b) Where there remains a genuine and outstanding question of interpretation of a provision in the 1938 Act, the directive may be used to aid interpretation.

Damages for failure to implement the Directive   1A–08

In *Francovich*[12] the European Court held that a Member State could be liable in damages to an individual for failing to implement a directive. Three conditions must be met:

1. the directive must be designed to create rights for individuals;
2. it must be possible to identify the content of those rights from the provisions of the directive; and
3. it is necessary to establish that the failure to implement the directive caused the loss suffered.

In the case of the Trade Marks Directive, the mandatory provisions satisfy the first two conditions. Whether the third is satisfied will be a question of fact in each case.

In a suitable case therefore, damages should be available for loss caused by the United Kingdom's failure to implement the Directive. Since the very life blood of a trade mark is the ability to stop infringers, an action against the state for damages will be very much the last resort.

---

[10] Para. 8 of the Judgment [1990] 1 E.C.R. 4135 at 4159; [1992] 1 C.M.L.R. 305 at 322.
[11] See in *Webb*, n. 9 above, Glidewell L.J. at 57, Beldam L.J. at 61 and Lord Keith at 939–940.
[12] Cases C-6 and 9/90 *Francovich v. Italy* [1991] I E.C.R. 5357; [1993] 2 C.M.L.R. 66 (E.C.J.).

CHAPTER 2

THE DEFINITION OF TRADE AND SERVICE MARKS

1. A MARK

2–02 "Mark"

ILLUSTRATION 1. See also *Smith Kline & French Laboratories' ("Cimetidine")* [1991] R.P.C. 17. The colour pale green was adopted for particular pharmaceutical preparations in order to distinguish them from other products and accordingly it was a trade mark; (the application was rejected on other grounds; see *post*, para. 8–61).

ILLUSTRATION 4. Add: *Esquire v. Roopanand* has been reversed on appeal: [1991] R.P.C. 425 (Sup. Ct. of S.A.). Noted *post*, para. 14–12.

FOOTNOTE 3: *"Coca-Cola"* reported at [1986] R.P.C. 421; [1986] 1 W.L.R. 695.

2–03 *Phrases, proverbs and slogans*

FOOTNOTE 4: The Court of Appeal has suggested, *obiter* and without argument, that registration of a slogan is possible, *Sinenide v. La Maison Kosmeo* (1928) L.T. 365 at 367.
  Moreover, the Privy Council in *"Pub Squash"* likewise considered that a slogan may be protectable in passing-off: [1981] R.P.C. 429 at 490.
  "Have A Break" has now been reported: [1993] R.P.C. 217.
  For a rather more liberal approach to the registration of phrases, see: *"I Can't Believe It's Yogurt"* [1992] R.P.C. 533 (B.o.T.). The mark was to be used on its own, without any other trade mark; as seen on a pot of yogurt the public would take the phrase as a brand name.
  Even if a slogan-type mark is registered, it may be difficult to show use of the mark as a trade mark, whether by the proprietor or by an alleged infringer. See *Unidoor v. Marks & Spencer* [1988] R.P.C. 275, where the principal use of the mark "Coast to Coast" was as a slogan on T-shirts.

2. USED OR PROPOSED TO BE USED

2–04 Used or proposed to be used

FOOTNOTES 14 AND 16: In *"Macy's"* [1989] R.P.C. 546, "use" in the U.K. was established by the operators of "Macy's" department store in New York by (1) the marking of goods for export (s.31), and (2) the importation of marked goods (following *Panhard et Levassor*).

Use in relation to goods or services

2–06

Amend the last sentence of §2–06 in the main work to read:

"So also, if foreign advertisements for services are to be relied upon as use, they must relate to services to be performed in the United Kingdom, the real use being that of a service mark."

In *"Dee"* [1990] R.P.C. 159 the Court of Appeal dismissed three appeals by retailers for various marks as service marks in respect of "retail services" and emphasised that the criteria which have to be satisfied if a mark is to qualify as a registrable service mark are:

(1) there must be a business providing the service or services in respect of which registration is sought;
(2) that service or services must be provided for money or money's worth;
(3) the proprietor of the mark must be connected in the course of business with the provision of that service or those services;
(4) the proprietor of the mark must use or propose to use the mark to indicate his connection in the course of business with the provision of that service or those services.

The service must be charged for separately and as such in order to fall within the statutory definition (*per* Slade L.J. at 180). All the constituents of the "retail services" relied on were ancillary to and part and parcel of the function of trading in goods. The position would have been different had the applicants been able to establish the fact that within their stores they were engaged in the business of providing any identifiable services for money or money's worth.

"Dee" was followed in *Tool Wholesale Holdings (Pty.) v. Action Bolt (Pty.)* [1991] R.P.C. 251 (Sup. Ct. of S.A.).

See also *"Gideons International"* [1991] R.P.C. 141; dissemination of bibles was not a service provided for money or money's worth.

See also *"Kodiak"* [1990] F.S.R. 49. The use of "Kodak" on T-shirts was   2–07
not use as a trade mark in relation to those goods; rather it was use in relation to films and plates.

Use of a mark on delivery notes and on invoices delivered long after sale constitutes use of the mark in the course of trade and in relation to the goods: *"Cheetah"* [1993] F.S.R. 263.

Illustration 2.   Add: In Ireland a more liberal view is taken: a free publication constitutes goods, the proprietor is in trade, so he is trading in the goods: *"Golden Pages"* [1985] F.S.R. 27.

3. REPRESENTATION TO BE CONVEYED BY THE MARK

2–14   *"Trade"*

See *"Kodiak"* [1990] F.S.R. 49, *ante*, para. 2–07.

FOOTNOTE 40:   See also *"Update"* [1979] R.P.C. 166, illustration 2, § 2–07 in the Main Work.

2–19A   *Provision of services*

See *ante*, para. 2–06.

2–21   **More than one business connected with goods or services**

The applicant was held not to be the proprietor of the mark applied for in circumstances where he was licensed (under an arrangement "founded heavily on personal contact and good faith") to assemble in the United Kingdom the goods to be marked (including locally sourced components) by the opponents, who at all times supplied the "vital control box". In addition, the opponents had requested the applicants to register the mark in the United Kingdom in the name of the opponents with the applicants as registered user: *"Sidewinder"* [1988] R.P.C. 261 (Regy.).

FOOTNOTE 56:   For another case of a manufacturer being entitled to a mark, see *"Sabatier"* [1993] R.P.C. 97 (Regy.). On its application to rectify, the manufacturer sought substitution of its name for that of the importer as proprietor. The mark was expunged, the manufacturer being free to make a fresh application for registration.

CHAPTER 3

THE REGISTER OF TRADE MARKS AND THE TRADE MARKS BRANCH OF THE PATENT OFFICE

3–01   **The Register**

Since April 1991 the addresses of the Trade Marks Registry at the Patent Office have been:

(1) Cardiff Road, Newport, Gwent NP9 1RH;
(2) 25 Southampton Buildings, London WC2A 1AY.

In practical terms the Trade Marks Registry has moved to Newport, but it retains a presence in central London. *Ex parte* hearings are often conducted by videolink between London and Newport, *inter partes* hearings are seldom so conducted.

5. INSPECTION OF THE REGISTER

Agency   3–17

For an unusual case where it was held that the agent had never been properly authorised and that a notice of opposition had no effect, see "*Bystander*" [1991] R.P.C. 279.

CHAPTER 4

REGISTRATION OF TRADE AND SERVICE MARKS

2. THE REGISTRAR'S DISCRETION

Nature of the Registrar's discretion   4–08

"Queen Diana" was used as a trade mark for Scotch whisky for 15 years. The Registrar refused registration under Rule 16. On appeal, the application was allowed. The mark did not fall within the rule, there being no "Queen Diana" and the mark was not likely to indicate royal patronage: "*Queen Diana*" [1991] R.P.C. 395 (B.o.T.).

3. PROCEDURE ON APPLICATION TO REGISTER

Consents   4–18

The Registry has allowed a consent to be withdrawn, holding that the initial giving of consent does not estop a party from later withdrawing the consent and entering an opposition: see "*Benji*" [1988] R.P.C. 251, where consent was given initially without the benefit of legal advice. This approach is consistent with the fact that consent cannot be the end of the matter since the Registry also has to take the interests of the public into account. See also § 10–08 in the Main Work.

4–20   Registrar to hear applicant before refusing the application

It is not proper for the Registrar to take into account material which has come to light following the hearing and upon which the applicants have not had an opportunity of commenting: *"Country Classics"* [1993] R.P.C. 524 (B.o.T.).

4–21   Second application for same mark

FOOTNOTE 64A: *Unilever* reported at [1987] R.P.C. 13.

4. OPPOSITION TO REGISTRATION

4–30   Opposition to registration

A mandatory injunction was granted to require withdrawal of an opposition where it was contrary to the terms of an agreement between the parties: *Sport International v. Hi-Tec Sports (No. 2)* [1990] F.S.R. 312.

4–31   (1) Procedure and evidence

Where matters raised before the Registry and the High Court are substantially the same (which may, for example, arise where opposition and passing-off proceedings are concurrent) then a stay of the proceedings in the Registry may be ordered to avoid multiplicity. For an unusual case where the Registry refused a stay but the High Court granted one by way of interlocutory injunction: see *Sears v. Sears Roebuck* [1993] R.P.C. 385 (since upheld on appeal, but the appeal is as yet unreported).

5. APPEALS FROM THE REGISTRAR

4–41   Appeal to Board of Trade

Quaere whether the Board of Trade has a fresh discretion in reviewing the exercise of discretion by the Registrar. The tribunal left the issue open in *"Queen Diana"* [1991] R.P.C. 395 (B.o.T.).

Although an appeal is a rehearing, an appellate tribunal will place great weight on a decision of the Registrar in relation to such practical matters as "goods of the same description", confusing similarity and the inherent nature of the mark. The decision will be reversed only where the Tribunal is satisfied that the Registrar is wrong: *"Bensyl"* [1992] R.P.C. 529 (B.o.T.).

Service out of the jurisdiction 4–45

Rule 13 applies to the service of documents on an applicant, who has no place of business in the United Kingdom, on an appeal to the High Court under section 18(7). Accordingly, service of an originating notice of motion by the opponent on the applicant's agents (who had been notified as the address for service on form TM8 in the opposition, as required by Rule 13) was good service: *Johnson & Johnson's Application* [1991] R.P.C. 1.

CHAPTER 5

CLASSIFICATION OF GOODS AND SERVICES; ASSOCIATION OF MARKS

1. THE CLASSES

Effect of classification 5–05

Services

There are only eight classes for services and there can be particular difficulties in choosing the right specification of services for a service mark. To ensure that a service mark proprietor obtains sufficient protection, it is prudent to consult the new classification of services issued by the Trade Marks Registry. The services which many proprietors want to cover will not fit into just one of the rather specific categories listed in the classification.

2. ASSOCIATED MARKS

Where a mark has been accepted only on condition that it is associated **5–08** with another mark, registration is not complete until the Registrar has duly marked the registrations as associated and has entered the mark to be registered in the association volume of the register.

So, in a case where the Registrar had failed to complete the registration of a mark owing to a clerical error and the applicant subsequently assigned two marks with which it was to be associated, the completion of the registration became impossible. The marks could not thereafter be associated without infringing the rights of the assignee. The applicant could not complain because it had made the completion impossible by entering into the assignment: "*Keds*" [1993] R.P.C. 72.

MARKS FOR "TEXTILE" AND THE MANCHESTER BRANCH OFFICE

2. THE MANCHESTER BRANCH OFFICE

7–02   As from April 15, 1991, and by virtue of The Patent Office (Address) Rules 1991 (S.I. 1991 No. 675), the address of the Manchester Branch of the Trade Marks Registry of the Patent Office has been: c/o Companies House, 75 Mosley Street, Manchester M2 3HR.

CHAPTER 8

WHAT MARKS MAY BE REGISTERED

2. ESSENTIAL PARTICULARS—SECTION 9(1)

"(c) An invented word or invented words"

8–26   *Examples of words held to be "invented"*

"*Exxate*": [1986] R.P.C. 567.

8–28   *Examples of words held not to have been invented*

"Fantastic Sam's" for hairdressing services (following "Solio"): "*Fantastic Sam's*" [1990] R.P.C. 531 (Regy.).
"Lite-Line" for particular dairy products: "*Lite-Line*" [1991] R.P.C. 390 (Regy.).
"Rijn Staal" (meaning Rhine steel) for chemical products used in steelmaking: "*Rijn Staal*" [1991] R.P.C. 400 (B.o.T.).
"2000 Two Thousand" for gin: "*2000 Two Thousand*" [1992] R.P.C. 65 (Regy.).
"Family Assurance Society" in a device for life assurance and investment management services: "*Family Assurance Society*" [1992] R.P.C. 253.

(d) Words having no direct reference to the character or quality of the goods

Words having "direct reference to character or quality" **8–31**

"Au Printemps" rejected for clothing. It had a direct reference to clothing intended for wear in the spring and in view of the aptness of the mark for normal description, registration in Part A or Part B would trespass on the legitimate freedom of other traders: "*Au Printemps*" [1990] R.P.C. 518 (Regy.).

"Lite-Line" rejected for particular dairy products. "Lite" was the phonetic equivalent of "Light". In any event the Registrar was entitled to rely on general knowledge as to the meaning and usage of "lite" (applying "*Heavenly*" [1967] R.P.C. 306 at 310): "*Lite-Line*" [1991] R.P.C. 390 (Regy.).

"Rijn Staal" (meaning Rhine steel) rejected for chemical products used in steelmaking. The mark had a reference to the quality and character of the goods. The translation did not prevent it being "direct": "*Rijn Staal*" [1991] R.P.C. 400 (B.o.T.).

"2000 Two Thousand" rejected for gin. Numbers were commonly used for a wide range of different purposes and could not be said to have no direct reference to the character or quality of the goods: "*2000 Two Thousand*" [1992] R.P.C. 65 (Regy.).

"Family Assurance Society" in a device for life assurance and investment management services: "*Family Assurance Society*" [1992] R.P.C. 253.

Words having no "direct reference to character or quality" **8–32**

"Weathershields" accepted for sliding roofs and the like for motor vehicles. The purpose of the goods was to give an option to be open to the weather, not to be shielded from it: "*Weathershields*" [1991] R.P.C. 451.

"Next", for tobacco and other goods in class 34, accepted as having no direct reference to the character or quality of the goods but rejected in the absence of use as "one of those words which would facilitate use in advertising slogans and the like" (applying "*Always*" [1986] R.P.C. 93): see "*Next*" [1992] R.P.C. 455 (B.o.T.).

Lists (Geographical names) **8–36**

"Rijn Staal" (meaning Rhine steel) rejected for chemical products used in steelmaking: "*Rijn Staal*" [1991] R.P.C. 400 (B.o.T.).

"Cos" for wine rejected as the phonetical equivalent of "Kos", an island in the southeast Aegean Sea known for the production of white and red wines: "*Cos*" [1993] R.P.C. 67.

Surnames **8–37**

See *post*, para. 8–54.

(e) Other distinctive marks

8–39 Date at which the mark must be distinctive

See also "*Lite-Line*" [1991] R.P.C. 390 (Regy.), *post*, para. 8–40.

8–40 Definition of "distinctive"

Section 9(3)(b) provides: "by reason of the use of the trade mark *or of any other special circumstances*, the trade mark is in fact adapted to distinguish as aforesaid" (emphasis added). These words were considered in "*Laura Ashley*" [1990] R.P.C. 539 (B.o.T.), *post*, para. 8–57. The applicants sought to rely on use of the mark in relation to other goods. It was held that "other circumstances" do include use for other goods, but the use will only weigh significantly if the goods are close in kind.

See also "*Lite-Line*" [1991] R.P.C. 390 (Regy.). An earlier registration for the same goods, which had inadvertently been allowed to lapse, did not constitute a special circumstance. A mark must be distinctive at the date of application.

In an attempt to register "Cos" for wine, it did not assist that the applicant had registered the mark "Cos D'Estournel" for the same goods without disclaimer: "*Cos*" [1993] R.P.C. 67 (Regy.).

8–41 Inherent and *de facto* distinctiveness

In a case that went on appeal to the Board of Trade the applicants sought registration of the mark "Colorcoat" in Part A in respect of steel sheet and strip, all having a coloured protective coating of plastic or paint. They had for some time a registration for the mark in Part B. The appeal was dealt with on the basis that the mark was now wholly distinctive in fact. The appeal failed; other traders might want to use the words "colour" and "coat", or something similar, and the privilege should not be conferred where it might require honest men to look for a defence: "*Colorcoat*" [1990] R.P.C. 511 (B.o.T.).

It is right to consider what other traders might legitimately want to do in the absence of any present factual distinctiveness of the mark: "*Budget*" [1991] R.P.C. 9 (B.o.T.).

"Weathershields" was not a mark other traders might legitimately desire to use for soft tops, sun tops, sliding roofs and folding roofs and it was inherently adapted to distinguish. Furthermore, the evidence showed that the mark had in fact become distinctive: "*Weathershields*" [1991] R.P.C. 451.

FOOTNOTE 78:   Add: Lord Simonds's reasoning in respect of a Part A mark applies also to a Part B mark: "*York*" [1984] R.P.C. 231 at 255.

8–42 Evidence of distinctiveness

For another case in which a survey was found to be unconvincing, see

Smith Kline & French Laboratories' ("Cimetidine") [1991] R.P.C. 17, *post*, para. 8–61.

Laudatory epithets

8–46

"Fantastic Sam's" rejected for hairdressing services having regard to the laudatory significance of "Fantastic" and non-distinctive "Sam's": *"Fantastic Sam's"* [1990] R.P.C. 531.

"Budget" rejected for car hire services despite factual distinctiveness. The word might reasonably be used to promote almost any goods or services: *"Budget"* [1991] R.P.C. 9 (B.o.T.).

Name of the goods

8–49

See also *"Weathershields"* [1991] R.P.C. 451, *ante*, para. 8–41. The opponents contended unsuccessfully that the mark was the name of goods not comprehended within the specification and that, consequently, registration was prohibited by Rule 19.

Purely descriptive terms

8–50

See also *"Colorcoat"* [1990] R.P.C. 511 (B.o.T.), *ante*, para. 8–41.

"Family Assurance Society" in a device for life assurance and investment management services: *"Family Assurance Society"* [1992] R.P.C. 253. Though the mark was factually distinctive, registration was only allowed on a disclaimer of all the words.

Geographical names

8–52

FOOTNOTE 13 (omitted from the Main Work): *"Dan River"* [1962] R.P.C. 157 at 162; mark registered in U.S. – where the only Dan River is – but still refused. As to natural monopolies, see the *"Appollinaris"* cases, cited at n. 14 in the Main Work, and the *"Karlsbader Wasser"* case (1912) 29 R.P.C. 162. More recently, in an unreported case, the Buxton Corporation was permitted to register "Buxton" for mineral waters on evidence that by long use the mark was distinctive of water from the mineral springs at Buxton, and that the corporation controlled them all. In the *"Karlsbad"* and the *"Buxton"* cases, an undertaking was required that the mark would be used only for natural water from the springs concerned. See also *"Stilton"* [1967] R.P.C. 173. (More a case of an historical monopoly perhaps.)

Surnames—Office practice

8–54

"Laura Ashley", as dominant feature of a device, rejected under the Registrar's published rules of practice: *"Laura Ashley"* [1990] R.P.C. 539 (B.o.T.), *post*, para. 8–57.

"Sam's" (as part of the mark "Fantastic Sam's") an uncommon surname and, as a pet name, has another well known meaning; thus the Registrar accepted that in its ordinary signification it was not a surname (but application rejected on other grounds – *ante*, para. 8–28 and *ante*, para. 8–46): "*Fantastic Sam's*" [1990] R.P.C. 531 (Regy.).

"Jenny Wren" allowed in Part A for articles of clothing without evidence of use and subject to a disclaimer to the exclusive use of the surname "Wren". The name was recognisably a "nursery name" and fell within section 9(1)(d): "*Jenny Wren*" [1991] R.P.C. 385 (B.o.T.).

8–55 Lists of word marks

Accepted words

"Jenny Wren" for clothing: "*Jenny Wren*" [1991] R.P.C. 385 (B.o.T.), *ante*, para. 8–54.

"Photo-Scan" for surveillance apparatus, not being or incorporating photographic apparatus: "*Photo-Scan*" [1987] R.P.C. 213 (B.o.T.).

"Weathershields" for soft tops, sun tops, sliding roofs and folding roofs: "*Weathershields*" [1991] R.P.C. 451, *ante*, para. 8–41.

8–56 *Refused words*

"Colorcoat" for steel sheet and strip: "*Colorcoat*" [1990] R.P.C. 511 (B.o.T.), *ante*, para. 8–41.

"Au Printemps" for clothing: "*Au Printemps*" [1990] R.P.C. 518 (Regy.), *ante*, para. 8–29.

"Fantastic Sam's" for hairdressing services: "*Fantastic Sam's*" [1990] R.P.C. 531 (Regy.).

"Budget" for car hire services: "*Budget*" [1991] R.P.C. 9 (B.o.T.).

"2000 Two Thousand" for gin: "*2000 Two Thousand*" [1992] R.P.C. 65 (Regy.).

"Next" for tobacco and other goods in class 34: "*Next*" [1992] R.P.C. 455 (B.o.T.).

"Black N' Red" for stationery articles: "*Black N' Red*" [1993] R.P.C. 25 (Regy.).

"Cos" for wine: "*Cos*" [1993] R.P.C. 67.

8–57 Devices

"The Solid Fuel Advisory Service", presented in four lines, three colours and particular script for advisory services rejected. The words were descriptive and the colours would be seen as mere decoration: "*Solid Fuel Advisory Service*" [1990] R.P.C. 535 (Regy.).

An application to register a device including the words "Laura Ashley" in a device for goods in class 28 without evidence of use was rejected. The words were prima facie incapable of distinguishing and, if disclaimed, left no residue. Furthermore, the use of the words alone by another trader might infringe: "*Laura Ashley*" [1990] R.P.C. 539 (B.o.T.).

"Rijn Staal" (meaning Rhine steel), including a device, rejected for chemical products used in steelmaking. So dominating were the words that a disclaimer to the words would not do; there would be no readily discernable residue: "*Rijn Staal*" [1991] R.P.C. 400 (B.o.T.).

Application to register a device mark comprising the word "Budget" between two parallel lines rejected – without the word the lines had no significance: "*Budget*" [1991] R.P.C. 9 (B.o.T.).

Marks comprising representations of an ingot for joss paper removed from the register in Singapore on evidence that they were common to the trade: *Cheng Kang v. Sze Jishian* [1992] F.S.R. 621 (High Ct., Singapore).

A pastoral landscape rejected for dairy products: *Union Laitiere Normande's* [1993] R.P.C. 87 (Regy.).

Devices descriptive of the goods   8–60

ILLUSTRATION 4.   The second *Unilever* case is reported at [1987] R.P.C. 13. The first attempt at registration created no issue estoppel, since each application dealt with the question of distinctiveness at its own date.

Get-Up as a Trade Mark   8–61

An application to register the colour pale green as a trade mark for particular pharmaceutical preparations was rejected. Held, a single colour for a medicinal tablet is not distinctive in law; furthermore, the colour had not been shown to be distinctive in fact: *Smith Kline & French Laboratories' ("Cimetidine")* [1991] R.P.C. 17.

The applicants sought to register a mark consisting of an external label sewn into and protruding from a structural patch pocket of a garment. Held, in the absence of evidence it was not distinctive or capable of distinguishing within the provisions of sections 9 and 10: "*Levi Strauss*" [1991] R.P.C. 441.

FOOTNOTE 25A: "*Coca-Cola*" reported at [1986] R.P.C. 421; [1986] 1 W.L.R. 695.

Initials and other letters   8–64

NEW ILLUSTRATION 8.   In "*Exxate*" [1986] R.P.C. 567, the objection was taken by the Registrar that the mark was the phoentic equivalent of 'X8' and unregistrable according to the practice set out in the Registry Work Manual. An appeal succeeded on the basis that no one else would want to use 'X8' in relation to their goods, unlike "W & G" and "Ogee".

For a further recent illustration of Registry practice, see "*I.Q.*" [1993] R.P.C. 379. An application for registration of the letters "I.Q." was refused because they were not clearly pronounceable as a word.

Use or registration abroad   8–68

See also "*Au Printemps*" [1990] R.P.C. 518 (Regy.), *ante*, para. 8–29. The mark had been used mainly in Paris and only to a limited extent in the United Kingdom. Registration refused.

3. MARKS REGISTRABLE IN PART B OF THE REGISTER

8–76   Practice under section 10

"Pound Puppies" for toy puppies, allowed on appeal since those words would not be the natural way that honest traders would describe toy puppies which cost a pound: "*Pound Puppies*" [1988] R.P.C. 530 (B.o.T.).

"Brut de Mer" for fish, refused, since it meant "straight from the sea" and would restrict the freedom of foreign traders to use ordinary descriptive words of their language on goods exported to this country: "*Brut de Mer*" [1989] R.P.C. 555.

"Fantastic Sam's" rejected for hairdressing services having regard to laudatory significance of "Fantastic" and non-distinctive "Sam's" (applying "*Torq-set*" [1959] R.P.C. 344): "*Fantastic Sam's*" [1990] R.P.C. 531 (Regy.).

"*Rijn Staal*" [1991] R.P.C. 400 (B.o.T.), *ante*, para. 8–57. With evidence of use, the position might be different.

"Next" rejected for tobacco and other goods in class 34 in the absence of use. Once it appears that the question is whether registration might trespass on the legitimate freedom of other traders, the reasons for refusal in Part A apply also to refusal in Part B: "*Next*" [1992] R.P.C. 455 (B.o.T.).

"Primasport" allowed for hosiery; it was a coined word and registration would not be to the detriment of members of the public (applying "*Always*" [1986] R.P.C. 93): "*Primasport*" [1992] F.S.R. 515.

"*I Can't Believe It's Yogurt*" [1992] R.P.C. 533 (B.o.T.). The phrase was allowed in Part B because it would not interfere with what other traders would reasonably wish to do.

"*Cos*" [1993] R.P.C. 67 (Regy.), *ante*, para. 8–36: "Cos" refused for wine in the absence of very extensive use.

Union Laitiere Normande's Application [1993] R.P.C. 87 (Regy.). A pastoral landscape rejected for dairy products; with evidence of use, the position might be different.

"*The Glenlivet*" [1993] R.P.C. 461 (B.o.T.). "The Glenlivet" allowed for water without evidence of use because the applicants had a substantial reputation under the mark in relation to whisky and there was a close association between whisky and water.

"*Magic Safe*" [1993] R.P.C. 470 (B.o.T.). "Magic Safe" refused for safes as being laudatory.

"*Country Classics*" [1993] R.P.C. 524 (B.o.T.). "Country Classics" refused for clothing. A number of other traders were using the mark.

See also the following: "*Budget*" [1991] R.P.C. 9 (B.o.T.), *ante*, para. 8–46.

Smith Kline & French Laboratories' ("Cimetidine") [1991] R.P.C. 17, *ante*, para. 8–61.

"*Levi Strauss*" [1991] R.P.C. 441, *ante*, para. 8–61.
"*Lite-Line*" [1991] R.P.C. 390 (Regy.), *ante*, para. 8–40.
"*Solid Fuel Advisory Service*" [1990] R.P.C. 535 (Regy.), *ante*, para. 8–57.
"*2000 Two Thousand*" [1992] R.P.C. 65 (Regy.), *ante*, para. 8–56.

Functions of the Board of Trade   8–80

In "*Sea Island Cotton*" [1989] R.P.C. 87, an application was made to the Board of Trade to expunge certification marks on three main grounds:

(1) the proprietors were no longer competent to certify;
(2) there had been failures to observe the provisions of the regulations;
(3) the registration of the marks was no longer to the public advantage.

In the result, whilst finding that the proprietor had been, for some periods, not competent to certify, that there had been some breaches of the regulations and that the established breaches of the regulations were not to the public advantage, it had not been shown that any member of the public had suffered and, owing to extenuating circumstances, the marks were not expunged.

CHAPTER 9

DISCLAIMERS

1. REQUIREMENT OF DISCLAIMER

Section 14 of the 1938 Act   9–01

An offer to disclaim non-distinctive parts of a mark may not be sufficient to render the mark registrable. The correct approach is to balance the respective importance of the distinctive and non-distinctive parts. If the non-distinctive parts overwhelm the distinctive parts, the mark is unregistrable: "*Merit*" [1989] R.P.C. 687, a decision of Whitford J. from 1983.

It is wrong to consider whether a disclaimer is required before a conclusion has been reached as to whether or not the trade mark is prima facie registrable: "*Superwound*" [1988] R.P.C. 272 (B.o.T.).

The words "Family Assurance Society" were required to be disclaimed in a device for life assurance and investment management services: "*Family Assurance Society*" [1992] R.P.C. 253. The application was proceeding on evidence of acquired distinctiveness and this made it all the more important that the public should know the extent of the applicant's rights.

2. Effect of Registration with Disclaimer

9–04   Effect of registration with disclaimer

New Illustration 3.   In *"Merit"* [1989] R.P.C. 687, Whitford J. expressed the view, *obiter*, that there might be circumstances in which a rival trader, although not infringing a device mark *per se*, might infringe the device mark plus a word, irrespective of the fact that there was a disclaimer of that word. In that case, an offer to disclaim *"Merit"*, admittedly prima facie non-distinctive, was not sufficient to render the mark registrable, since the non-distinctive parts overwhelmed the distinctive parts.

Chapter 10

RESTRICTIONS ON REGISTRATION

1. Conflict with Earlier Marks

10–02   Sections 11 and 12(1)

In *"Macy's"* [1989] R.P.C. 546, the Registry followed *Bali* saying that the likelihood of confusion for section 11 had to be decided on the basis of use and not reputation, hence distinguishing *"Ovax"/Smith Hayden*. The opponents operated *"Macy's"* department store in New York. Although they could show use of their unregistered *"Macy's"* mark by the marking of goods for export and for import, that use extended only to clothing. Thus an application for clothing was refused and an application for watches was allowed.

Footnote 8:   Registration was refused where the export of a single pump to the U.K. was held to be sufficient "use" in the U.K. to found a s.11 objection, *"Sidewinder"* [1988] R.P.C. 261.

10–05   Likelihood of confusion

Under section 12, as under section 11, it may be appropriate to take into account any special dangers arising from confusion: *"Terbuline"* [1990] R.P.C. 21 (B.o.T.). See also the Main Work, para. 10–42 (as to s.11), and para. 4–08 (nature of the Registrar's discretion).
See also *"Univer"* [1993] R.P.C. 239.

Consents of proprietors   10–08

A consent may be withdrawn and opposition entered, which is consistent with the Registry's role in protecting the public: *"Benji"* [1988] R.P.C. 251.

2. SECTION 12(1)—GOODS OR SERVICES OF THE SAME DESCRIPTION OR ASSOCIATED

The tests to be applied   10–12

FOOTNOTE 70:   For an illustration of such a comparison, see *"Fingals"* [1993] R.P.C. 21 (Regy.). Wines and restaurant services were "associated".

Goods of the same description   10–15

In *Williams & Humbert v. I.D.V.* [1986] F.S.R. 150, Whitford J. thought that sherry and a blend of white rum and passion fruit juice "might well" be goods of the same description.
Wound dressings included goods of the same description as analgesic preparations: *"Inadine"* [1992] R.P.C. 421.
Soaps included medicated soaps which were goods of the same description as pharmaceutical preparations: *"Bensyl"* [1992] R.P.C. 529 (B.o.T.).
Cardiovascular preparations for use in treating humans, and for supply only on prescription by a registered medical practitioner, were goods of the same description as veterinary preparations and substances: *"Univer"* [1993] R.P.C. 239.

Goods not of the same description

Held, *obiter*, T-shirts not goods of the same description as footwear: *"Kodiak"* [1990] F.S.R. 49.
Pharmaceutical fungicides for humans were not goods of the same description as fungicides for use in agriculture: *"Invicta"* [1992] R.P.C. 541 (B.o.T.).

3. SECTION 12(2)—CONCURRENT USE

Section 12(2)   10–16

In allowing registration of the mark "Star" under section 12(2) despite opposition under sections 11 and 12 based upon the mark "Spar", the Registrar attached weight to the market reality that the opposed marks and goods were kept at a distance from each other, rather than to the wide range of possibilities for "normal and fair use": *"Star"* [1990] R.P.C. 522 (Regy.).

10–21   "Or other special circumstances"

Prior registration of two marks of a similar kind by other proprietors did not constitute a special circumstance sufficient to justify registration. It involved too much supposition to say that persons must be used to distinguishing between the marks: "*Terbuline*" [1990] R.P.C. 21 (B.o.T.).

5. SECTION 11—DECEPTIVE OR SCANDALOUS MARKS

10–26   Section 11

FOOTNOTE 58:   See also "*Guntrum*" [1990] R.P.C. 27. The Registrar applied "*G.E.*" in allowing registration of a mark which had become confusing through no fault of the applicants.

10–31   Mark deceptive as to quality of goods or business

An application for "Photo-Scan" was remitted to the Registry for amendment of the specification of goods after the Board of Trade did not uphold a section 11 objection provided the mark was used on non-photographic goods: "*Photo-Scan*" [1987] R.P.C. 213 (B.o.T.).
"Pound Puppies" was allowed in Part B. Normal and fair use of the mark would not be likely to confuse the public into thinking that the toy puppies sold under it cost one pound, particularly in the light of evidence which showed that nobody could buy them for that price: "*Pound Puppies*" [1988] R.P.C. 530 (B.o.T.).

10–39   National and imperial emblems, etc.

See also "*Queen Diana*" [1991] R.P.C. 395 (B.o.T.), *ante*, para. 4–08.

CHAPTER 11

VALIDITY AND RECTIFICATION OF THE REGISTER

11–04   Exceptions to section 13

(a) *Fraud*

Under the equivalent Australian provision, a mark was held to have been obtained by fraud where the applicant stated to the Registry that the mark was used and was proposed to be used, when that statement was known by the applicant to be false: *The Ritz Hotel v. Charles of the Ritz* [1989] R.P.C. 333.

NEW ILLUSTRATION 1. The plaintiffs secured registration of a mark comprised of Chinese characters meaning "life nourishing wine". In response to a request from the United Kingdom Registrar for a transliteration of the characters and whether they had any meaning, only the phonetic equivalent, "Yomeishu", was provided. Held, there was a serious issue of fraud to go to trial: *Yomeishu Seizo v. Sinma Medical Products* [1991] F.S.R. 278 (H.C., Singapore).

1. WHO MAY APPLY: PERSONS AGGRIEVED

NEW ILLUSTRATION 3. *Lever v. Sunniwite* (see illustration 2 in the Main **11–08** Work) was considered and distinguished in "*Kodiak*" [1987] R.P.C. 269 (C.A.), where the applicant for "Kodiak" for boots claimed to be a person aggrieved in relation to all goods for which "Kodak" was registered, *viz.*: all articles of clothing. The fact that the applicant might claim relief wider than that to which he was ultimately found to be entitled was held to be irrelevant, since *locus standi* was conferred if an application was blocked by the presence on the register of an allegedly unused mark. "Person aggrieved" was not to be unduly limited.

NEW ILLUSTRATION 4. In a case where the parties had operated under various agreements for many years, including a registered user agreement, the proprietor wrote to the user to contend that the agreements were void under Article 85 of the Treaty of Rome and that use of the marks which were the subject of the agreements must cease. The user disputed this conclusion, contending that the agreements were still in force, but also applied to register the marks itself and to rectify the register by having the marks owned by the proprietor removed. Held, in relation to the application to rectify, the user was not a person aggrieved. Furthermore, by operating under the agreements for many years the user was estopped from claiming what amounted to ownership of the marks: "*Job*" [1993] F.S.R. 118 (Regy.).

FOOTNOTE 35: For another, perhaps unduly restrictive, approach, see "*Bach Flower Remedies*" [1992] R.P.C. 439 (Regy.). The registered proprietors had asserted passing-off against the applicant for rectification but contended successfully they had no objection to the use of the mark as a description in the title of the applicant's publications. Accordingly, he was not a person aggrieved.

FOOTNOTE 37, *re* "a fixed intention to trade": In "*Concord*" [1987] F.S.R. 209, a person undecided or left in doubt as to whether to proceed to use a mark or not due to the existence of a pertinent registration could be a "person aggrieved".

2. RECTIFICATION UNDER SECTION 32

11–16   Section 32—The nature of the section

As a matter of English law (and leaving aside questions of restraint of trade and Article 85 of the EEC Treaty) "no challenge clauses" in trade mark delimitation agreements are not unenforceable as being contrary to the public interest: *Apple Corps v. Apple Computer* [1992] F.S.R. 431.

11–19   (3) Abandonment

See also *Image Enterprises v. Eastman Kodak* [1989] F.S.R. 353, a case from South Africa where the judge indicated that whilst a lengthy period of non-use of a mark might indicate an intention to abandon, mere non-use was not usually enough. Other factors would be required, such as the proprietor's liquidation or a declared intention not to use the mark.

11–22   (4) Mark becoming deceptive

FOOTNOTE 76:   See also *New South Wales Dairy Corporation v. Murray Goulburn* [1991] R.P.C. 144 (Full H.C. of Australia) for a decision under the similar provision, section 28 of the Trade Marks Act 1955 (Australia) and an interesting consideration of the circumstances which might constitute "blameworthy conduct".

11–37   Effect of delay in making the application

NEW ILLUSTRATION 1.   M commenced proceedings against A in 1980 to rectify the register by removal of a mark under sections 26 and 32. For nine years M took no step in the proceedings. In 1990, M commenced further proceedings under section 26 alleging no bona fide use for a period of five years or longer prior to the application. A sought to have the earlier proceedings struck out on the grounds of inordinate and inexcusable delay and prejudice. Held, declining to strike out but ordering that all the proceedings be heard together as soon as possible, A had failed to show that there was a substantial risk that a fair trial of the earlier proceedings was not possible; furthermore, the later proceedings were not confined to the five years before 1990 and could cover the period covered by the earlier actions: *"High Life"* [1991] R.P.C. 445.

3. RECTIFICATION FOR NON-USE

11–38   Section 26

NEW ILLUSTRAITON 1.   Apple Corps sought an interlocutory injunction to restrain Apple Computer from acting in breach of a trade mark delimitation agreement anywhere in the world. Apple Computer contended that in such a case the *Cyanamid* rules did not apply. Held, granting an injunction, that subject to the need for caution in granting injunctions to restrain foreign proceedings, the *Cyanamid* principles did apply: *Apple Corps v. Apple Computer* [1992] R.P.C. 70.

FOOTNOTE 11: In "*Bon Matin*" [1989] R.P.C. 537, Whitford J. decided that the five-year period is measured from the date when the mark is actually put on the register.

Use in relation to goods   11–39

See also "*Kodiak*" [1990] F.S.R. 49, *ante*, para. 2–07.

Evidence   11–41

It is not an abuse of process to allege non-use without inquiry of the plaintiff: *Gala of London v. Chandler* [1991] F.S.R. 294.

For a case where a prima facie case of no bona fide intention to use was made out, see "*Palm*" [1992] R.P.C. 258. It was nine years since the date of application and seven years since registration, yet there was no evidence of any preparatory steps to market any goods the subject of the registration.

FOOTNOTE 26: Add: the reasoning in "*Revue*" was applied in "*Flashpoint*" [1988] R.P.C. 561.

"Bona fide"   11–45

The fact that the motive for hurried use of a registered mark was to prevent it being vulnerable to an action for non-use was held not to be relevant to the issue of bona fides: "*Concord*" [1987] F.S.R. 209, applying "*Electrux*". It was also held that the use had only been a temporary operation, not embarked upon in a genuine attempt to establish trading under the mark and was not a bona fide use within section 26.

See also "*Kodiak*" [1990] F.S.R. 49, *ante*, para. 2–07. It was further held that the use was not bona fide in relation to T-shirts in that the use was for the ulterior purpose of advertising other goods.

Special circumstances in the trade   11–47

See also *Re Jellied Beef* [1993] F.S.R. 484 (German Court of Appeal). The ban on a product by a national law which was later found to be in contravention of Community law considered to be a justification for non-use for more than five years.

6. Procedure on an Application for Rectification under Sections 26, 27(4), 28(8), 32 and 33

11–69 **Intervention by third parties**

See also "*McGregor*" [1979] R.P.C. 36; and note, *post*, para. 11–71 in relation to proceedings before the court.

11–70 **Application to the court**

A respondent to rectification proceedings successfully sought interrogatories as to the goods in relation to which the applicant had used the marks in issue: *Parfums Yves Saint Laurent v. The Ritz Hotel* [1990] F.S.R. 36 (C.A.) (Hong Kong).

11–71 **Parties**

A party with an interest in proceedings for rectification before the court may be allowed to intervene: "*Tradam*" [1990] F.S.R. 200.

Parallel proceedings for rectification of the same mark were commenced in England and Scotland by related companies. The respondents sought to add as additional respondents to the English proceedings the pursuers in Scotland to ensure that full discovery was given and so that they would be bound by any decision of the English court. Held, there was jurisdiction to add them as respondents under R.S.C. Ord. 15, r. 6 and in the interests of justice and limitation of costs and expenditure of court time, they should be added: "*Dirt Magnet*" [1991] F.S.R. 136.

7. Correction and Cancellation of Entries at the Proprietor's Request under Section 34

11–86 **Instances of alterations**

For a recent illustration of the refusal to allow an alteration on the ground that it would alter the essential element of the mark, see *Seaforth Maritime* [1993] R.P.C. 72 (Regy.).

COMMUNITY LAW

2. THE FREE CIRCULATION RULE

The rule stated   12–03

Where goods have been put on the market in a Member State under one mark the rights of the proprietor under a different mark have not been used on first marketing and are not exhausted: "*Cheetah*" [1993] F.S.R. 263.

"Specific subject-matter"   12–05

In *Hag II*, *post*, para. 12–09, the European Court of Justice has clearly recognised the essential value of trade marks in enabling enterprises to gain customers by the quality of their goods or services, and for that purpose a trade mark must constitute a guarantee that all products bearing it have been manufactured under the supervision of a single enterprise.

The European Court has restated that the *specific subject-matter* of a trade mark is:

> "to grant the owner the right to use the mark for the first marketing of a product and, in this way to protect him against competitors who would like to abuse the position and reputation of the mark by selling products to which the mark has been improperly affixed".

The *essential function* of a trade mark is:

> "to give the consumer or final user a guarantee of the identity of the origin of the marked product by enabling him to distinguish, without any possible confusion, that product from others of a different provenance".

It is doubtful that trade marks can be regarded now as somehow less worthy of protection than other industrial property rights.

Repackaging   12–06

FOOTNOTE 30:   See also Case IV/32.877 *The Community v. Bayer AG* [1992] F.S.R. 201; [1992] 4 C.M.L.R. 61, *post*, para. 12–19.

12–07 Re-affixing

But the court will not assume that the use of different marks in different territories amounts to a disguised restriction on trade in the absence of evidence.

So where herbicide was marketed under the name "Puma" in Belgium and "Cheetah" in the United Kingdom, an application was successfully made for summary judgment to restrain the use of the mark "Cheetah" in relation to the product imported from Belgium. The mere fact that it was possible to buy in Belgium and sell in the United Kingdom at a profit was not sufficient evidence of the use of the marks as a disguised restriction on trade: "*Cheetah*" [1993] F.S.R. 263.

12–09 Marks of "Common Origin"

The European Court of Justice has reversed its decision in *HAG* (*Van Zuylen v. Hag* – now referred to as *Hag I*) in Case 10/89 *S.A. CNL-SUCAL NV v. HAG GF AG* (referred to as *Hag II*) [1991] F.S.R. 99; [1990] I E.C.R. 3711; [1990] 3 C.M.L.R. 571. After the decision in *Hag I* (for the facts of which, see the Main Work) Van Zuylen Frères was purchased by a Swiss company which disposed of most of VZF's coffee business but leaving the "Hag" trade marks. The firm was transformed into a subsidiary of its new owner trading under the name SA CNL-SUCAL NV ("HAG Belgium"). HAG Belgium then began to supply "Hag" coffee to the German market whereupon HAG GF AG ("HAG Germany") sued in Germany for infringement of trade mark. Held, (on a reference to the European Court) Articles 30 and 36 of the EEC Treaty do not preclude the exercise by a party of trade mark rights to oppose the importation of similar goods marked with the same or a confusingly similar mark,

> "even though the mark under which the disputed products are imported originally belonged to a subsidiary of the enterprise which opposes the importation and was acquired by a third enterprise as a result of the expropriation of that subsidiary".

The actual judgment in *Hag II* leaves a number of issues unresolved. For example, does the common origin doctrine apply if a mark is divided voluntarily otherwise than as part of a deliberate market sharing agreement? It is suggested that it probably does. What happens if two marks with a common origin are confusingly similar in one territory but not in another? Those who wish to investigate further are encouraged to read the Opinion of Advocate-General Jacobs [1990] I E.C.R. 3711 at 3725; [1990] 3 C.M.L.R. 571 at 575.

Before *Hag II* was decided, a common origin argument based on *Hag I* failed on the facts in *Tayto (Northern Ireland) Ltd. v. McKee* [1991] 3 C.M.L.R. 269 (High Court, Northern Ireland). The "Tayto" mark was devised by a trader in the Republic of Ireland. An agreement in 1956 gave the use of the "Tayto" name, together with selling and production rights in

Northern Ireland, to the plaintiff company. In due course the plaintiff registered "Tayto" in the United Kingdom. Meanwhile, both traders flourished and competed in each other's territories but, so far as use of the "Tayto" mark was concerned, both kept to their respective territories. By the time the United Kingdom and Ireland joined the E.C., the restrictive elements of the 1956 agreement had ceased to be operative.

The defendant imported crisps into Northern Ireland from the Republic and was sued for both passing-off and for trade mark infringement. It was held that the doctrine in *Hag I* did not apply because the marks had never been in common *ownership*; nor were they the result of a subdivision of trade mark rights by agreement.

For another pre-*Hag II* decision, see the decision of the German Federal Supreme Court in *Re "Klint"* [1988] 1 C.M.L.R. 340.

3. Articles 85 and 86

What type of breach gives a defence?   12–15

Footnote 62:   Our courts have now demonstrated a fairly robust attitude to Euro-defences; see, *e.g. Duracell v. Ever Ready* [1989] R.P.C. 731, defences under Arts. 86 and 30 to 36 were struck out.

"May affect trade between Member States"   12–17

Digital Equipment Corp. v. LCE Computer Maintenance (Mervyn Davies J., May 22, 1992, unreported); an Article 86 Euro-defence to a copyright claim was struck out on the basis of no effect on trade between Member States.

Footnote 71:   See also *Sport International v. Hi-Tec Sports (No. 2)* [1990] F.S.R. 312.

Scope of Article 85   12–19

(6) *Agreement to minimise confusion*

· See also *The Community v. Syntex Corporation* [1990] 4 C.M.L.R. 343; [1990] F.S.R. 520, Article 85(1) is applicable to trade mark delimitation agreements in cases where it is not evident that the holder of an earlier trade mark could have recourse to national law to prevent the holder of a later mark from using it in one or more Member States.

(12) *Dealership and distribution agreements*

A blanket prohibition on repackaging may be contrary to Article 85. Thus, a provision in a sales contract for dental products that they may be supplied to a third party only in unopened form was contrary to Article 85.

Furthermore, a provision in a sales contract prohibiting export may be contrary to Article 85: as may a term stating that the goods are intended for distribution in only one territory and that their resale abroad may, in the country concerned, be prohibited because they contravene registration regulations and may infringe industrial property rights: *The Community v. Bayer AG* [1992] F.S.R. 201; [1992] 4 C.M.L.R. 61.

4. PROCEDURAL QUESTIONS

12–20 The court may allow a party in proceedings before it to submit documents obtained from the other party on discovery to the Commission. See *Apple Corps v. Apple Computers* [1992] F.S.R. 389; [1992] 1 C.M.L.R. 969. But *cf. Bonzel v. Intervention* [1991] R.P.C. 43.

CHAPTER 13

ASSIGNMENT AND DEVOLUTION OF TRADE AND SERVICE MARKS "REGISTERED USERS"

2. THE NATURE OF GOODWILL

13–09 **What constitutes goodwill**

Although goodwill is undoubtedly a valuable form of property, it is probably not capable of precise definition. Moreover, the concept of goodwill depends upon the context concerned. For instance, an accountant might want to value goodwill: in the case of a company, he could do so by subtracting from its net worth (as measured by share value) the net value of all its assets, both tangible and intangible (other than trade marks and trade names).[1] What is left over he could call the value of the goodwill. But that "goodwill" may well include elements which would not be material for other purposes; for instance, a high-risk research-based company has value because of the hope of future valuable inventions. That value would be included as part of the goodwill value in the accountant's exercise but it is not part of the goodwill generated within the trade or among customers, which is the more conventional view of goodwill. Goodwill arising merely from the absence of effective competition (*e.g.* for a unique shop in a particular area)

---

[1] Not necessarily an easy exercise; things like patents are notoriously difficult to value.

likewise would be relevant to a valuation exercise but irrelevant from a trade mark or passing-off point of view.

Currently there are moves within the accountancy profession to include the goodwill associated with important company brands as separate items in the balance sheet of the company. Whilst this can be done in theory, there are dangers both from an accounting point of view and from a legal perspective. The accountancy danger is that such an exercise could lead to overvaluing a company, not only because there would be a risk that the goodwill of the company generally might be overvalued.[2]

The legal danger is that businessmen will tend to regard the goodwill of the brand as an asset which can be used, borrowed against or otherwise dealt with just as in the case of any other asset. But goodwill poses special problems: the general common law rule that it cannot be divorced from the business,[3] although now relaxed in some cases, is founded on an innate feeling about the nature of goodwill itself. Thus, unless there are very special licensing provisions, the goodwill of a brand is not a suitable security for a loan – the lender would not be sure of his security.

Judicial statements of the nature of goodwill 13–09A

Various judicial statements of the nature of goodwill have been given. The elements of goodwill (for the purposes of landlord and tenant law) were colourfully described by Scrutton L.J. as follows[4]:

> "A division of the elements of goodwill was referred to during the argument and appears in Mr. Merlin's book [on the Landlord and Tenant Act] as 'cat, rat and dog' basis. The cat prefers the old home though the person who has kept the house leaves. The cat represents that part of the customers who continue to go to the old shop, though the old shopkeeper has gone; the probability of their custom may be regarded as an additional value given to the premises by the tenant's trading. The dog represents that part of the customers who follow the person rather than the place; these the tenant may take away with him if he does not go too far. There remains a class of customer who may neither follow the place nor the person, but drift away elsewhere. They are neither a benefit to the landlord nor to the tenant, and have been called 'the rat' for no particular reason except to keep the epigram to the animal kingdom. I believe my brother Maugham has introduced the rabbit,[5] but I will leave him to explain the position of the rabbit. It is

---

[2] What is left after subtraction of the "brands"?

[3] See above.

[4] *Whiteman Smith Motor Company v. Chaplin* [1934] 2 K.B. 35 at 42; *cf. Mullins v. Wessex Motors* [1947] W.N. 316. Not all these animals would be relevant in passing-off. The dog is really the one who counts – for it is he who wants to deal with a particular enterprise. It is he who would not only be deceived but misled by a false representation that the new enterprise was really the old one.

[5] He also introduced a mouse!

obvious that the division of customers into 'cat, rat and dog' must vary enormously in different cases and different circumstances."

13–09B Other aspects of goodwill

The goodwill of a partnership is an asset which is saleable upon break-up of the partnership.[6] Goodwill may be the subject of a *Mareva* injunction.[7]

Although goodwill is a form of property, the law does not protect that property from any form of attack. It is the essence of competition that one man may attract business from a competitor. In the absence of lawful contractual restraints, it is the tort of passing-off[8] which protects goodwill. Passing-off only prevents invasions of goodwill by damaging misrepresentations.

13–09C Ownership of goodwill

Ordinarily, a number of traders will be concerned with goods before they reach the ultimate consumer. Questions arise in these circumstances as to who is the owner of the goodwill. Similar questions arise when two parties originally connected with goods become estranged. The law is not always easy to determine in this kind of case. Normally, the inquiry is simply one of fact; of whom is the mark distinctive?[9] Thus, in the case of manufactured goods the public normally looks to the manufacturer (whether foreign or not and whether or not they actually know his name) as the man responsible for the goods under the mark. But this is not always so on the facts, as in a case where the public regard the vendor (*e.g.* a supermarket using its own name) as the person responsible for getting the goods made. The question may be complicated further by contractual arrangements made between the rival claimants to goodwill. What is clear is that the law will not use any fiction or equitable doctrine to aid one side or the other.[10] A number of cases considered in Chapter 16 take the form of passing-off actions but can also be regarded as disputes over ownership of goodwill.[11] There are cases where goodwill has been divided lawfully or shared. In such cases the result is that those entitled to exploit the goodwill cannot interfere with each other, but all have a right against third party pirates.[12]

---

[6] *Hill v. Fearis* [1905] 1 Ch. 466.
[7] *Darashah v. UFAC (U.K.)*, (C.A.), *The Times*, March 30, 1982.
[8] Chapter 16 where further discussion involving the nature of goodwill can be found.
[9] See *Oertli v. Bowman* [1959] R.P.C. 1 at 5 *per* Viscount Simmonds.
[10] *Ibid.*
[11] See §§ 16–23, 16–33, 16–89, 16–91, 16–92 in the Main Work.
[12] See §§ 16–60, 16–89, 16–90 in the Main Work.

4. Use by Persons other than Registered Proprietor

Termination of registered user agreement   13–32A

C entered into certain registered user agreements with S which included restrictions as to the manner in which the marks might be used. S committed certain breaches of those restrictions and C purported to terminate. S contended that the breaches had been spent when the termination notices were served. *Held*, the breaches were not capable of remedy and they had not been spent. The purpose of the restrictions was to protect the value to C of their marks; use other than as permitted might lead to them becoming deceptive. Furthermore, relief from forfeiture was not available: *Crittal Windows v. Stormseal (UPVC) Window Systems* [1991] R.P.C. 265.

Chapter 14

THE DEFINITION OF INFRINGEMENT

1. General: Section 4

Whether rights limited to trade mark or service mark use   14–05

"Treat Size" was not used as a trade mark in relation to confectionery: *Mars v. Cadbury* [1987] R.P.C. 387.

At the interlocutory stage "extreme doubt" was expressed as to whether the defendants were using the slogan "Coast to Coast" as a trade mark on the front of T-shirts: *Unidoor v. Marks & Spencer* [1988] R.P.C. 275.

See also *Games Workshop v. Transworld Publishers* [1993] F.S.R. 705 (C.A.) where it was held that there was a seriously triable issue that the title on a series of books was used as a trade mark.

"In the course of trade"; "in connection with the provision of any services"   14–06

In *Levi Strauss v. Kimbyr Investments* (Williams J., High Court of New Zealand, June 28, 1993 [1994] F.S.R. 335) Levi Strauss succeeded in proving infringement of their "tab" mark in respect of jeans. Much of the evidence of confusion related to "post-sale" confusion, in that witnesses considered jeans as they would appear being worn after sale. At the point of sale, cardboard labels and the like were sufficient to eliminate confusion unless the purchaser took only a cursory glance at the labels. After sale, those labels were removed, leaving the tab in the seam of a rear pocket of the jeans.

The defendants argued that no infringement had occurred because the alleged deception or confusion had not occurred "in the course of trade", relying on a dictum of Lord MacMillan in *Aristoc v. Rysta* [1945] A.C. 68 at 97, where he said:

> " 'Trade' is no doubt a wide word but its meaning must vary with and be controlled by its context. A connection with goods in the course of trade in my opinion means ... an association with the goods in the course of their production and preparation for the market. After goods have reached the consumer they are no longer in the course of trade. The trading in them has reached its objective and its conclusion in their acquisition by the consumer."

The judge rejected the argument, characterising *Aristoc* as containing two main issues: first, whether it was permissible to register a mark which was not being used in the course of trade but only in repairs. Lord MacMillan's dictum related to this first issue, hence the defendants had taken it out of context. The second issue in *Aristoc* was whether there was a potential for confusion if the registration was granted. Relating to this second issue, Williams J. referred to examples of post-sale confusion relied upon by their Lordships and in particular, Lord MacMillan at 98 and 99 and Lord Wright at 103.

Williams J. also drew support from the decision of Whitford J. in *Levi Strauss v. Shah* [1985] R.P.C. 371, saying that it was implicit in the comments at 374 and 375 to 376 that post-sale confusion is relevant to the question of infringement.

See further, *post*, para. 17–17.

14–07   "In relation to goods"; in relation to services

Use of the word "Harrods" to advertise the defendant's former connection with the store was to identify the store and not any goods in it. Therefore, there was no use of the mark "Harrods" in relation to goods or in any trade mark sense: *Harrods v. Schwartz-Sackin* [1986] F.S.R. 490.

14–08   Use on wrappers, etc.

It is an infringement to use a mark on delivery notes and on invoices delivered long after sale: "*Cheetah*" [1993] F.S.R. 263.

14–12   Meaning of "visual representation": small size of mark

Esquire v. Roopanand has been reversed on appeal: [1991] R.P.C. 425 (Sup. Ct. of S.A.). A mark registered for a specification of goods including videotapes, was incorporated in the proprietor's recorded tapes so that when they were played, the mark appeared on the screen at intervals; and this feature was carried over into pirate tapes. In an action for infringement, held, on appeal, the ordinary viewer would regard the mark which appeared on the screen as referring to the pre-recorded tape. Accordingly there was a use of the trade mark in the form of a visual presentation on the television screen and it was use in the course of trade in relation to pre-recorded video cassettes. The defendants produced the video cassettes and sold them knowing and intending that they would be put to use and that that use would necessarily involve the visual presentation of the trade mark.

Locality of infringement   14–13

See also *L.A. Gear v. Gerald Whelan* [1991] F.S.R. 670. An attempt by a defendant to invoke Articles 21 or 22 of the Brussels Convention on the basis of pending proceedings in Ireland failed.

The registration must cover the goods or services in question   14–15

The test whether the goods alleged to infringe fell within the specification of goods was a question for the consumer and was not to be determined by expert scientific evidence: *Unilever v. Johnson Wax* [1989] F.S.R. 145, where a thick liquid lavatory cleaner was held not to fall within "common soap and detergents".

FOOTNOTE 47:   See also *Portakabin v. Powerblast* [1990] R.P.C. 471, *post*, para. 17–08. The defendants' contention, that their products were not buildings, was rejected; the plaintiffs' products were buildings and the defendants' products had the same essential features. Furthermore, in its advertising materials, the defendants had themselves described their products as portable shotblast "rooms".

2. SECTION 4(1)(*b*): "IMPORTING A REFERENCE"

Effect of paragraph (*b*) of section 4(1)   14–26

It now seems clear that an advertisement may be "issued to the public" even if it is only issued to a specialist class of the public, such as retailers in a particular trade. Hence, the issue of a manual containing a comparison chart to a network of independent distributors constituted the issue of an advertisement to the public: *Chanel v. Triton Packaging* [1993] R.P.C. 32 (C.A.).

It follows that the text of § 14–26 in the Main Work is wrong.

Importing a reference   14–27

In *Duracell v. Ever Ready* [1989] F.S.R. 71, the defendants advertised their battery by saying it "outlasted the equivalent sold by Duracell Batteries

Limited". That company owned the mark "Duracell". On motion it was held that "Duracell", with other words, was being used to refer to the plaintiff's goods. Hence infringement was arguable, since the reference to the goods in *Pompadour* was implied, whereas here it was express.

Newsgroup Newspapers v. Mirror Group Newspapers [1989] F.S.R. 126, was a stronger case on the facts. The mark "Sun", registered for newspapers, was alleged to have been infringed in an advertisement where the mark appeared underneath "Yes, Prime Minister" in juxtaposition to the masthead of *The Daily Mirror* underneath "No, Prime Minister". Since the defendant intended to refer to its own newspaper, it was difficult to see how "The Sun" could refer to the business, rather than the newspaper. It was also argued that there was no infringement because there was no appropriation of goodwill. That was held to be irrelevant.

3. SAVINGS AND EXCEPTIONS

14–29   Limitation for use on the genuine goods: section 4(3)(*a*)

In order to establish a connection in the course of trade, it is not always necessary that the goods have actually been placed on the market by the proprietor or a registered user.

Thus, in *Accurist Watches v. King* [1992] F.S.R. 80, a registered user of a trade mark owned by the plaintiffs had watches made for it bearing the mark under contracts with the defendants. The contracts contained reservation of title clauses against default of payment by the user. When the user became insolvent the defendants retook possession of the watches and proposed to sell them. They were sued for infringement of trade mark by the plaintiffs. Held, section 4(3)(*a*) provided a complete defence to the action.

14–30   Parallel imports

The matter now appears to depend upon the intention of the proprietor when the mark is applied: *Colgate-Palmolive Ltd. v. Markwell Finance Ltd.* [1989] R.P.C. 497 (C.A.). Did the proprietor apply the United Kingdom registered trade mark or was a mark applied to goods which was neither used nor proposed to be used in the United Kingdom? In practice, not even the proprietor is likely to have a ready answer to this question, particularly if goods are supplied to many countries from a single production source. In particular, how is a parallel importer to find the answer, other than when he is sued? *Colgate* gives two clues: the language on the packaging and a difference in quality.

This situation is in marked contrast to the position within the European Union.

In *Colgate* it was accepted that there had never been an application of the relevant United Kingdom trade marks to toothpaste manufactured in Brazil. The "Colgate" mark applied to the goods in Brazil was a Brazilian mark and neither used nor intended to be used in the United Kingdom. Hence the sale of Brazilian "Colgate" toothpastes in the United Kingdom resulted in infringement of the United Kingdom registered trade mark.

CHAPTER 15

THE ACTION FOR INFRINGEMENT

2. THE PLAINTIFF'S TITLE

Registered user as plaintiff   15–06

However, in *Levi Strauss v. French Connection* [1982] F.S.R. 443, Falconer J. struck out the second plaintiff registered user, leaving the registered proprietor as sole plaintiff.

3. COMMENCEMENT OF THE ACTION

In what court an infringement action should be commenced   15–10

Where an infringer is committing infringements in more than one E.C. country at the same time, the prospective plaintiff needs to consider the effect of the Brussels Convention, implemented by the Civil Jurisdiction and Judgments Act 1982.

The principal aim of the Convention is to avoid conflicting judgments in different contracting states by providing a set of rules for deciding where actions should be brought. The general rule is that a defendant should be sued in his domicile, but that general rule is qualified by other rules to cope, for example, with actions with more than one defendant, and with tort and contract actions.

Of particular relevance to registered trade marks is Article 16(4) which gives exclusive jurisdiction over matters relating to validity to the courts of the state where the marks are registered. Thus validity of a United Kingdom registered trade mark must be decided by a United Kingdom court. (The Act contains a special set of rules for deciding jurisdiction within the U.K.) Article 16(4) says nothing about infringement actions, which are therefore left to be dealt with under the general provisions, which retain a degree of flexibility. Whilst other jurisdictions see nothing unusual in deciding infringement in a different action to validity (*e.g.* Germany, in relation to patents), it certainly does seem odd to us in the United Kingdom.

The rules of the Convention are detailed and need to be interpreted carefully. However, judges are human and if a plaintiff can demonstrate a real connection with the jurisdiction in which he has chosen to sue then he is unlikely to be forced to litigate somewhere else. If there is to be a forum dispute, some advantage is obtained by starting the first set of proceedings.

4. DEFENCES

15–19   Defences

The question whether a counterclaim could constitute a defence to infringements committed before rectification is ordered was considered, but held not suitable to be determined on motion in *Gala of London v. Chandler* [1991] F.S.R. 294 (*cf. Williams & Humbert v. IDV* [1986] F.S.R. 150).

15–28   Trade marks of anterior date

The defence failed in *Portakabin v. Powerblast* [1990] R.P.C. 471, *post*, para. 17–08. The plaintiffs invoked section 30(2) and relied on anterior use of their marks, "Portakabin" and "Portasilo".

15–32   Section 8

A section 8(*b*) defence failed in *Mars v. Cadbury* [1987] R.P.C. 387, despite the fact that the defendants were not using "Treat Size" as a trade mark, neither was it use of a bona fide description of the character of the goods, since the defendant had built up some degree of distinctiveness.

15–33   Bona fide use

The question whether the test is objective or subjective arose for consideration in *Provident Financial v. Halifax Building Society* [1994] F.S.R. 81. Aldous J. felt constrained to follow *Baume v. Moore* [1958] R.P.C. 226, but pointed out that this may lead to the absurd result that an uninformed fool might have a defence under section 8 whereas the properly informed reasonable man would not.

15–37   "Importing any such reference"

See also *Portakabin v. Powerblast* [1990] R.P.C. 471, *post*, para. 17–08. The word "Portoblast" was being used as a trade mark and not as a description.

(4) Acquiescence, delay and consent

Representation by proprietor   15–45

See also *Portakabin v. Powerblast* [1990] R.P.C. 471, *post*, para. 17–08, where the defence failed on the facts.

False assertion of registration   15–54

For a case where the plaintiffs had, prior to registration of their mark, said that it was registered: *Compaq Computer v. Dell Computer* [1992] F.S.R. 93, *post*, para. 18–20. An injunction was not refused, following *Coles v. Need* [1934] A.C. 82.

See also *Intercontex v. Schmidt* [1988] F.S.R. 575.

5. THE RELIEF GRANTED

(1) Injunction

Form of injunction   15–63

More so than a trade mark, a registered service mark will sometimes only be used in a particular geographical area. An alleged infringer may consider rectification of the register in order to limit the geographical scope of the registration or argue that any injunction should be limited geographically. See, however, *Chelsea Man v. Chelsea Girl* [1987] R.P.C. 189, where the defendant failed to limit the injunction geographically.

Interlocutory application for an interim injunction   15–65

A plaintiff which abandons a motion or seeks to stand it to trial may be at risk as to costs in a case where the court considers, on the material the plaintiff has produced and what it must have known about the defendant, that it was not justified in launching the motion at all: *Kickers v. Paul Kettle* [1990] F.S.R. 436.

It is incumbent on a plaintiff who has been protected by an interlocutory injunction to proceed with the action with due diligence so as to limit as far as possible the period during which the defendant's liberty is restricted without there being any determination on the merits: *Newsgroup Newspapers v. Mirror Group Newspapers* [1991] F.S.R. 487.

Balance of convenience   15–66

See *post*, para. 16–102.

15–67   Compromise of interlocutory application

Where, however, the plaintiff is unwilling to fight his motion and seeks to stand the motion to the trial, the motion may be disposed of with an order for the defendant's costs in the cause: *Kodak v. Reed International* [1986] F.S.R. 477.

15–68   Interim injunction refused on account of delay

Delay of some five months whilst correspondence passed and without-prejudice negotiations were pursued was not such as to disentitle a large corporate plaintiff to an interlocutory injunction against a sole trader: *"Oxford" Marmalade* [1986] F.S.R. 527.

(3) Damages or profits

15–76   No distinction between infringement and passing-off

Note that VAT may be payable on any sum paid by way of settlement: *Cooper Chasney v. Commissioners of Customs and Excise* [1992] F.S.R. 298.

15–78   Onus of showing substantial damage lies on the plaintiff

In an action for infringement of trade mark and passing-off, the defendants consented to judgment. The plaintiffs brought an application for an interim payment and sought damages on a reasonable royalty basis and the costs of pursuing the foreign manufacturers. It was held, on appeal from a master, that it was not appropriate to award damages on a royalty basis at that stage. There was no reported authority for assessing damages on a royalty basis in an action for infringement of trade mark or passing-off and it was difficult to reconcile the proposition with the rule that not every infringing sale could be attributed to the plaintiff when assessing damages on a loss of sales basis. The legal costs of putting innocent foreign manufacturers on notice were reasonably foreseeable: *Dormeuil v. Feraglow* [1990] R.P.C. 449.

6. COSTS

15–88   Costs in the discretion of the judge

Note that the legal costs of putting innocent foreign manufacturers on notice were reasonably foreseeable and therefore recoverable as *damages: Dormeuil v. Feraglow* [1990] R.P.C. 449.

Unsuccessful party usually ordered to pay costs 15–89

In a passing-off case a further plaintiff was joined to deal with a question as to the ownership of the goodwill in a United Kingdom business. The defendants, who were unsuccessful in the action, were awarded their costs to the date of joinder. The plaintiffs were otherwise entitled to their costs of obtaining an injunction even if any damages awarded on the enquiry did not exceed any payment in. A letter written "without prejudice as to costs" offered too little and was too late: *Colgate Palmolive v. Markwell Finance* [1990] R.P.C. 197.

Offer by infringer 15–90

See *Colgate Palmolive v. Markwell Finance* [1990] R.P.C. 197, *ante*, para. 15–89.

7. APPEAL

Stay pending appeal 15–97

FOOTNOTE 77: Stay of interlocutory injunction pending appeal granted on the defendant's undertaking to pay 10 per cent. of profits into a joint account: *"Oxford" Marmalade* [1986] F.S.R. 527.

8. PRACTICE AND EVIDENCE

"Anton Piller", "Mareva" and similar orders 15–110

In applying for any *ex parte* order, but particularly in the case of *Anton Piller* orders, great care must be taken to ensure that all relevant matters are put before the court. For a recent case where failure to do so resulted in the order being set aside, an injunction granted to restrain use being made of information obtained and indemnity costs being ordered against the applicant: see *Naf Naf v. Dickens* [1993] F.S.R. 424. (For other cases of a similar kind in other areas, see *The Supreme Court Practice 1993*, Ord. 29.)

For further ancillary relief, see *Bayer v. Winter (No. 1)* [1986] F.S.R. 323 (order restraining a defendant leaving the jurisdiction and requiring delivery up of passports) and *Bayer v. Winter (No. 2)* [1986] F.S.R. 357 (information obtained pursuant to an *Anton Piller* order could be used to start actions in other jurisdictions in order to obtain protective measures).

Evidence of title 15–114

The reference to section 58 in the second paragraph and to section 57 in note 12 should be to sections 1(8) and 1(9) respectively, sections 57 and 58 having been repealed.

15–116 Trap orders

Trap orders are bound to involve an element of deception. The extent to which it is proper for a solicitor to participate, for example to ensure that a proper record is made of what occurs, is a matter for their professional body: *Marie Claire v. Hartstone* [1993] F.S.R. 692.

CHAPTER 16

THE ACTION FOR "PASSING-OFF"

1. FOUNDATION AND NATURE OF THE ACTION

16–01A "Unfair competition"

At the interlocutory injunction stage of *Associated Newspapers v. Insert Media* (see *post*, paras. 16–04, 16–08), in addition to passing–off, the plaintiff argued a separate and distinct cause of action to the effect that the law would prevent deliberate acts calculated to cause damage to the plaintiff's goodwill: based on *Emperor of Austria v. Day* (1861) 3 De G. F. & J. 217 and *Kingdom of Spain v. Christie* [1986] 1 W.L.R. 1120. Even without the benefit of full argument, this new cause of action was rejected: *Mail Newspapers v. Insert Media* [1987] R.P.C. 521.

16–02 Definition

See also *Reckitt & Colman v. Borden ("Jif")* [1990] R.P.C. 341 (H.L.) (see *post*, paras. 16–67, 16–77), where their Lordships reverted to the "classical trinity".
Lord Oliver at 406:

> "The law of passing-off can be summarised in one short general proposition – no man may pass off his goods as those of another. More specifically, it may be expressed in terms of the elements which the plaintiff in such an action has to prove in order to succeed. These are three in number.
>
> First, he must establish a goodwill or reputation attached to the goods or services which he supplies in the mind of the purchasing public by association with the identifying 'get-up' (whether it consists simply of a

brand name or a trade description, or the individual features of labelling or packaging) under which his particular goods or services are offered to the public, such that the get-up is recognised by the public as distinctive specifically of the plaintiff's goods or services.

Secondly, he must demonstrate a misrepresentation by the defendant to the public (whether or not intentional) leading or likely to lead the public to belief that the goods or services offered by him are the goods or services of the plaintiff ...

Thirdly, he must demonstrate that he suffers or, in a *quia timet* action, that he is likely to suffer damage by reason of the erroneous belief engendered by the defendant's misrepresentation that the source of the defendant's goods or services is the same as the source of those offered by the plaintiff."

Lord Jauncey at 416:

General law applicable to passing-off actions
"The basic underlying principle of such an action was stated in 1842 by Lord Langdale M.R. in *Perry* v. *Truefitt* (1842) 6 Beav. 66 at 73, to be: 'A man is not to sell his own goods under the pretence that they are the goods of another man ...' Accordingly a misrepresentation achieving such a result is actionable because it constitutes an invasion of proprietary rights vested in the plaintiff. However, it is a prerequisite of any successful passing-off action that the plaintiff's goods have acquired a reputation in the market and are known by some distinguishing feature. It is also a prerequisite that the misrepresentation has deceived or is likely to deceive and that the plaintiff is likely to suffer damage by such deception. Mere confusion which does not lead to a sale is not sufficient.

... it is not essential ... that the defendant should misrepresent his goods as those of the plaintiff. It is sufficient that he misrepresents his goods in such a way that it is a reasonably foreseeable conseqence of the misrepresentation that the plaintiff's business or goodwill will be damaged."

See also *Consorzio del Prosciutto di Parma v. Marks & Spencer ("Parma Ham")* [1991] R.P.C. 351 (C.A.), and in particular the following, *per* Nourse L.J., at 368:

"Although those speeches [Lord Diplock and Lord Fraser of Tullybelton in *Warnink v. Townend*, at 742 and 755] are of the highest authority, it has been my experience, and it is now my respectful opinion, that they do not give the same degree of assistance in analysis and decision as the classical trinity of (1) a reputation (or goodwill) acquired by the plaintiff in his goods, name, mark, etc., (2) a misrepresentation by the defendant leading to confusion (or deception), causing (3) damage to the plaintiff."

16–03   The House of Lords has since reverted to "the classical trinity": see *"Jif"*, *ante*, para. 16–02.

FOOTNOTE 11:   Definitive statements of the law are so often overtaken by subsequent events. When dealing with a case of so-called "reverse passing-off" the Court of Appeal, in *Bristol Conservatories v. Conservatories Custom Built* [1989] R.P.C. 455, preferred a conventional analysis of passing-off, albeit with unusual facts, expressing views about *"Advocaat"*, *viz.*: that the respective five probanda of Lords Diplock and Fraser are not cumulative; that Lord Fraser's probanda were stated in relation to the type of case he was considering and are not of universal application; and that it was not correct that passing-off was limited to "classic" cases and the "extended form" established in *"Advocaat"*.

16–04   Need for proof of damage

There may be no need for clear evidence of damage, even where the misrepresentation is that the plaintiffs must have authorised and taken responsibility for the defendants' activities if the parties are appealing to the same customers and the defendants intend to exploit the plaintiffs' goodwill: *Associated Newspapers v. Insert Media* [1991] F.S.R. 380 (C.A.) – distinguishing the case of *"Stringfellows"* [1984] R.P.C. 501 (C.A.), a case where little, if any, overlap existed and there was no attempt to trade on the plaintiff's goodwill.

Erosion of distinctiveness is a form of damage to goodwill which may be sufficient to maintain an action, provided the damage is actually caused by the misrepresentation.

So in a case where it was shown that the sale of "Elderflower Champagne" would lead people to believe that it was champagne, or in some way associated with it, passing-off was established. Erosion of the distinctiveness of the name champagne was a form of damage to the goodwill of the champagne houses: *Taittinger v. Allbev* [1993] F.S.R. 641 (C.A.).

The need for proof of damage presents special problems in any case of "character merchandising"; see §§ 16–08 and 16–64 in the Main Work and *post*, paras. 16–08 and 16–64.

FOOTNOTE 16:   See also *Blazer v. Yardley* [1992] F.S.R. 501, *post*, para. 16–08. In a case where there was no direct overlap of trade but it was accepted there was a serious issue to be tried that the defendants' products might be associated with the plaintiffs; held, refusing an injunction, use of the plaintiffs' goodwill by definition causes injury to the plaintiff and lays open that goodwill to damage by the actions of the defendants; but the risk of that damage pending trial was outweighed by the damage that would be caused to the defendants.

16–08   Field of activity

Relief granted: see also *Associated Newspapers v. Insert Media* [1991]

F.S.R. 380 (C.A.); the plaintiffs were granted an injunction to restrain the unauthorised insertion of advertising material into their newspapers.

Relief refused: see also *Blazer v. Yardley* [1992] F.S.R. 501; the plaintiffs, who had for many years used the mark "Blazer" in relation to their goods and business in clothing, refused an interim injunction to restrain the marketing of "English Blazer" toiletries.

Reputation   16–10

FOOTNOTE 52:   Add: *Chelsea Man v. Chelsea Girl* [1987] R.P.C. 189, upheld on appeal.

Where the plaintiff had done nothing to indicate its connection with the   16–11
mark "Coast to Coast", instead using it mainly as a slogan on T-shirts, Whitford J. expressed the view at the interlocutory stage that the plaintiff would have difficulty in establishing reputation: *Unidoor v. Marks & Spencer* [1988] R.P.C. 275.

Time needed to acquire reputation   16–12

Where the defendant advertises his goods and workmanship by showing photographs of the plaintiff's goods and workmanship, the defendant may, simultaneously, be generating goodwill and reputation for the plaintiff and making a misrepresentation sufficient to found a passing-off action: see *Bristol Conservatories v. Conservatories Custom Built* [1989] R.P.C. 455.

A period of six months was insufficient to establish a reputation in the name "The Gold AM" for a radio programme comprising "Golden Oldies": *County Sound v. Ocean Sound* [1991] F.S.R. 367.

FOOTNOTE 55:   See also *BBC v. Talbot* [1981] F.S.R. 228; *Elida Gibbs v. Colgate-Palmolive* [1983] F.S.R. 95; *My Kinda Bones v. Dr. Pepper's Store* [1984] F.S.R. 289; *Marcus Publishing v. Hutton-Wild* [1990] R.P.C. 576.

Territorial considerations: the "Crazy Horse" problem   16–18

FOOTNOTE 80:   Hughie Green failed to establish any goodwill in New Zealand relating to his "Opportunity Knocks" series broadcast in England, despite having (some rather thin) evidence that a proportion of people in New Zealand would have seen the series in England, when visiting or living here: *Green v. Broadcasting Corporation of New Zealand* [1989] R.P.C. 469 (C.A. of N.Z.). (The appeal to the Privy Council did not concern passing-off: [1989] R.P.C. 700.)

FOOTNOTE 90:   See also *Tan-Ichi v. Jancar* [1990] F.S.R. 151 (Hong Kong High Ct.).

2. DIRECT MISREPRESENTATION AS TO BUSINESS OR GOODS

16–25   Direct false statement

FOOTNOTE 21:   See also *Associated Newspapers v. Insert Media* [1991] F.S.R. 380 (C.A.).

16–27   System of advertising

See also "*Pub Squash*" [1981] R.P.C. 429 (P.C., N.S.W.), noted in the Main Work, § 16–02.

16–28   Passing-off one quality of goods for another

The Consortium of Parma ham producers alleged that the sale of pre-sliced Parma ham amounted to passing-off because the process of pre-slicing and packing affected the taste and quality of the product so that it could no longer be described as "Parma ham". The claim was struck out. It was necessary for the Consortium to show that the pre-sliced Parma ham was different not only in degree, but in kind – in other words, that it no longer was Parma ham. That made it necessary to define Parma ham in order to be able objectively to identify the difference between the two products. The Consortium could not do this (*per* Leggatt L.J. at 380–382): *Consorzio del Prosciutto di Parma v. Marks & Spencer ("Parma Ham")* [1991] R.P.C. 351 (C.A.). (See also *post*, para. 16–31, for other aspects of the case.)

FOOTNOTE 31:   See also *Colgate-Palmolive Ltd. v. Markwell Finance Ltd.* [1989] R.P.C. 497 (C.A.), where it was proved that the Brazilian "Colgate" toothpastes were inferior to the U.K. "Colgate" toothpastes.

FOOTNOTE 35:   Whether a multinational business is conducted in substance as only one business so that the goodwill is shared by the group is a matter of fact to be determined in each case. Thus, where a group conducted separate businesses in bananas in the U.K. and Europe under the mark "Fyffes", it could not found a claim that there was in substance only one business and that the goodwill was shared by all members. After severance of the different businesses, the owners of the U.K. business sought an interlocutory injunction restraining the owners of the European business from taking any action to prevent them marketing bananas in Europe under the mark. The owners of the European business countered by alleging that the marketing of bananas on the European mainland by the owners of the U.K. business under the mark "Fyffes" would amount to passing-off, infringement of trade mark and a breach of contract. The court granted an injunction in favour of the European business, restraining the owners of the U.K. business from marketing bananas on the European mainland under the mark: *Fyffes v. Chiquita Brands International* [1993] F.S.R. 83.

3. IMITATIONS OF TRADE OR SERVICE MARK, GET-UP, ETC.

Shared reputation
16–31

FOOTNOTE 48:   It may be important to determine the precise scope of the reputation enjoyed. The Consortium of Parma ham producers failed to establish that the sale of pre-sliced Parma ham amounted to a misrepresentation because the crown of the Consortium, which confirmed authenticity, was thereby removed, or because the ham had not been sliced in front of the customer. The defendants were selling sliced Parma ham as sliced Parma ham: *Consorzio del Prosciutto di Parma v. Marks & Spencer ("Parma Ham")* [1991] R.P.C. 351. (See also *ante*, para. 16–28.)

See also *Consejo Regulador De Las Denominaciones "Jerez-Xeres Sherry" Y "Manzanilla De Sanlucar De Barrameda" v. Mathew Clark* [1992] F.S.R. 525. The plaintiffs were granted an interlocutory injunction to restrain the defendants from selling their product in bottles marked "Original Pale Cream" and "Classic Aperitif – a select blend of Premium British Sherry and Fine Fortified Wines from Spain". The plaintiffs made much of the similarity between the name and that of "Croft Original Pale Cream", the most successful sherry of the last decade.

Use of the name or description of the goods
16–34

See also *Marcus Publishing v. Hutton-Wild* [1990] R.P.C. 576 (C.A.). Far too little had been done by the plaintiffs to establish a goodwill in the descriptive name "Leisure Week" for a new magazine.

A period of six months was insufficient to establish a reputation in the name "The Gold AM" for a radio programme comprising "Golden Oldies": *Country Sound v. Ocean Sound* [1991] F.S.R. 367.

Secondary meaning not acquired while no competition
16–42

NEW ILLUSTRATION 5.   For many years the plaintiff had sold cigarette papers in three weights, each indicated by a colour on the packaging: red, blue and yellow. The defendant launched its own three weights of cigarette papers, whose packaging was readily distinguishable from the plaintiff's although they also used red, blue and yellow to indicate the three weights. Passing-off was alleged on the basis that: (a) the plaintiff's papers were never on display, being kept under the counter; and (b) that people would ask for a packet of "reds" and be supplied with the defendants' papers. The judge thought that it was by no means clear that a request for "reds" meant the plaintiffs' goods as opposed to papers of that weight. He also thought that any confusion could be avoided by the plaintiff's ensuring that their goods were put on display; interlocutory relief was refused: *Rizla v. Bryant & May* [1986] R.P.C. 389.

16–48   Geographical names

See also *Consejo Regulador De Las Denominaciones "Jerez-Xeres Sherry" Y "Manzanilla De Sanlucar De Barrameda" v. Mathew Clark* [1992] F.S.R. 525, noted *ante*, para. 16–31.

4. Business Names

16–50   Descriptive names

Illustration 4.   Add: "Furnitureland"/"Furniture City". The difference in the suffixes was held sufficient to avoid even an arguable case in passing-off: *Furnitureland v. Harris* [1989] F.S.R. 536.

16–52   Name suggesting a branch or agency

Footnote 34:   See also *Ewing (t/a Buttercup Dairy Co.) v. Buttercup Margarine Co.* [1917] 2 Ch. 1; 34 R.P.C. 232, (C.A.).

16–61   Title of periodical, book, film

Illustration 6.   For other cases where an injunction was refused, see: *Advance Magazine Publishing v. Redwood Publishing* [1993] F.S.R. 449. There was no arguable case that a magazine entitled *BBC Gourmet Good Food* would be confused with the title *Gourmet*.

County Sound v. Ocean Sound [1991] F.S.R. 367, *ante*, para. 16–34, a case involving the name of a radio programme.

Management Publications v. Blenheim Exhibitions Group [1991] F.S.R. 348 and 550 (C.A.). The plaintiffs argued that the public would think that the two publications *Management Today* and *Security Management Today* were connected. Held, arguable case in passing-off; injunction refused on the balance of convenience.

Marcus Publishing v. Hutton-Wild [1990] R.P.C. 576 (C.A.), *ante*, para. 16–34.

Tamworth Herald v. Thomson Free Newspapers [1991] F.S.R. 337. The plaintiff published the *Tamworth Herald* and a free sheet, the *Tamworth Herald Extra*. The defendants proposed to rename the *Tamworth Trader* the *Tamworth Herald and Post*. The mastheads looked different and would make it clear that the paper had been renamed. Held, no arguable case.

For a case where an injunction was granted, see *Morgan Grampian v. Training Personnel* [1992] F.S.R. 267. The plaintiffs published a series of titles including the expression "What's New In . . .". The defendants had used the title "Training Personnel", but changed it to "What's New In Training". An injunction was granted on the balance of convenience.

Names of fictional characters: "character merchandising"   **16–64**

This important topic more properly covers names and *likenesses* of fictional and *real* characters and should be read in particular association with § 16–08 (Field of activity) and § 16–04 (Need for proof of damage) in the Main Work.

In the case of *Mirage Studios v. Counter-Feat Clothing* [1991] F.S.R. 145, the plaintiffs were the owners of the copyright in the fictional humanoid turtle cartoon characters known as Teenage Mutant Ninja Turtles. Their business and income involved licensing the reproduction of the turtles under contracts which included quality control. The defendants, seeking to take the concept of the plaintiffs' turtles rather than their actual form, produced their own drawings of humanoid turtles and began to merchandise them. The plaintiffs alleged passing-off and sought an interlocutory injunction. The evidence showed that a substantial number of the buying public now expect and know that when a famous cartoon or television character is reproduced on goods, that reproduction is the result of a licence granted by the owner of the copyright or other rights in that character. Held, granting an injunction, that if the case were to go to trial the plaintiffs would establish their right in law to complain of passing-off.

The Vice-Chancellor found each of the elements of Lord Diplock's formulation of the tort in *"Advocaat"* to be made out on the evidence. There was a misrepresentation; the public would assume that the product was genuine and licensed; and it was plainly made by a trader in the course of trade to prospective customers. Further, and critical to the case, it would damage the plaintiffs in their business of copyright licensing. The plaintiffs would lose royalties and the depreciation of the image of their turtles might seriously reduce the value of the licensing right. Finally, that damage had occurred or would probably do so.

In finding passing-off, the Vice-Chancellor followed the Australian cases: *Children's Television Workshop v. Woolworth (New South Wales)* [1981] R.P.C. 187 and *Fido Dido v. Venture Stores* 16 I.P.R. 365. He considered that the English cases of *"Wombles"* [1977] R.P.C. 99, *Tavener Rutledge v. Trexapalm ("Kojak")* [1977] R.P.C. 275 and *Lyngstad v. Anabas* [1977] F.S.R. 62, did not touch the case where the plaintiff had a business in licensing copyright and observed (at 158) that perhaps different factors applied in such cases, though they might, given the change in trading habits, require reconsideration on a future occasion if the evidence before the court was different.

5. Imitation of Get-Up

In the *"Jif"* case, Reckett & Colman established that the *"Jif"* lemon-   **16–67**
shaped plastic container had acquired a secondary significance. The question then came down to whether Borden, in adopting containers having the most striking feature of the *"Jif"* get-up, had taken sufficient steps to

distinguish their products. It was found that they had not; this despite the fact that the Borden lemons did have labels which were marked "Realemon". The case can be understood in the light of the particular findings of fact; namely that for customers a crucial point of reference was the lemon shape and that virtually no attention was paid to the label. Shoppers had no reason to read the label or pay any attention to it in order to obtain the goods they required. *Reckitt & Colman v. Borden ("Jif")* [1990] R.P.C. 341 (H.L.). (See also *post*, para. 16–77.)

Borden deployed a number of arguments. First, they contended that a distinction must be drawn between a manufactured article itself, and the special trade insignia (such as get-up) used to designate its trade origin. The article itself could not constitute the special insignia of its own origin. Lord Oliver dealt with the argument by rejecting the suggestion that the container was an object in itself rather than part of the get-up. Lord Jauncey, who gave the other principal speech, adopted the more robust position that the shape and configuration of the article could be protected against deception and confusion. He concluded (at 426):

> "This principle [that no man may sell his goods under the pretence that they are the goods of another] applies as well to the goods themselves as to their get-up. A markets a ratchet screwdriver with a distinctively shaped handle. The screwdriver has acquired a reputation for reliability and utility and is generally recognised by the public as being the produce of A because of the handle. A would be entitled to protection against B if the latter sought to market a ratchet screwdriver with a similarly shaped handle without taking sufficient steps to see that the public was not misled into thinking that his product was that of A."

Borden also contended that mere confusion was not sufficient to found the cause of action; they argued that all that they had done was to adopt a descriptive device and that Reckitt & Colman were not entitled to relief simply because they had used the same device as descriptive of their own goods and had been the only people previously to adopt that description. This, of course, was not a novel proposition. It is well established that where a descriptive term is used, a plaintiff must show more than simply the sole use of it. He must show that it has acquired a secondary meaning not simply of the goods of that description, but also of goods of which he, and he alone, is the source. The difficulty facing Borden was that the trial judge had found as a fact that the "Jif" lemon container was so distinctive.

Reckitt & Colman for their part, accepted that they had to establish deception and confusion and argued that the crucial question is "What moves the public to buy?", a question taken from the judgment of Learned Hand J. in *Crescent Tool Co. v. Kilborn & Bishop* (1917) 147 F. 299. Although not expressly referred to in the speeches, it appears (particularly from the passage cited above from the speech of Lord Jauncey) that this was accepted. What a plaintiff has to do is to prove that it is deception which moves the public to buy the defendant's goods. If successful, the plaintiff has proved both the fact of misrepresentation and that the misrepresentation was operative.

See also *Weber-Stephen v. Alrite Engineering* [1992] R.P.C. 549 (Sup. Ct. of S.A.).

FOOTNOTE 83:   See also *Financial Times v. Evening Standard* [1991] F.S.R. 7. The *Financial Times* complained of the adoption by the *Evening Standard* of the colour pink for its financial section. Held, on an *ex parte* application, the question whether there was a real likelihood of confusion was ultimately for the court; here, confusion was very unlikely.

FOOTNOTE 91:   In *Kemtron v. Jimmy's* [1979] F.S.R. 86 (Hong Kong), the plaintiff managed to establish an arguable case in passing-off since there were some peculiarities in the plaintiff's get-up which were not dictated by function. *Cf. Komesaroff v. Mickle* [1988] R.P.C. 204 (Australia), where the judge thought that functional features of the plaintiff's moving sand features were not inherently distinctive of proprietary origin and hence that the plaintiff had to show acquired distinctiveness by long user. In cases of this type it ought to be relatively easy for a defendant to distinguish his goods (with the same get-up comprised of functional features) by the addition of his own, distinctive mark.

FOOTNOTE 92:   See also *Charles Church v. Cronin* [1990] F.S.R. 1. The plaintiff, a builder, sought to contend that the copying of a particular design of house could amount to passing-off. The claim was struck out. There was nothing capricious in the design; any distinctive features that the design had were part of the house.

6. PROOF OF LIKELIHOOD OF DECEPTION

Generally   16–72

Mere confusion is not enough; it is essential for the plaintiff's proprietary right and goodwill in the name in question to be made out: *Marcus Publishing v. Hutton-Wild* [1990] R.P.C. 576 (C.A.).

For a further illustration of this important point, see *County Sound v. Ocean Sound* [1991] F.S.R. 367, *ante*, para. 16–12, where it was emphasised (following *Marengo v. Daily Sketch* (C.A.), 1946, now reported [1992] F.S.R. 1) that before it is actionable, confusion has to be such as is caused by the defendant's misrepresentation that his goods or services are the goods of the plaintiff.

See also *Tamworth Herald v. Thomson Free Newspapers* [1991] F.S.R. 337, *ante*, para. 16–61. Confusion was already taking place because of the use of the word "Tamworth" by both the plaintiffs and defendants. The mere fact that after the defendants changed the title of their publication both would also be using the word "Herald", a word commonly used by newspapers, and that this might lead to mistakes, did not mean that there would be any misrepresentation.

See also the Main Work, § 16–30.

16–77 **All the circumstances to be considered**

In *Plix Products v. Winstone* [1986] F.S.R. 608, the Appeal Court in New Zealand felt it unnecessary to decide the question of passing-off, but indicated that, in the particular circumstances, there was little likelihood of confusion. The goods in question were a form of packaging for kiwi fruit. The evidence showed confusion on the part of some growers and some who worked in the packing sheds, because the respective parties' packaging were similar in colour and appearance. That evidence was not material, since the customers for the goods were those who owned the packing businesses. They were unlikely to be confused, because the goods were supplied in distinctive cartons or bags.

Surveys present special problems: see the Main Work, § 17–28. They were used to effect in *Reckitt & Colman v. Borden ("Jif")* [1990] R.P.C. 341 (H.L.), a *quia timet* action. The surveys conducted are summarised at 350.

7. DEFENCES

16–84 **Use of one's own name**

FOOTNOTE 60: See also the judgments of the Appeal Court in *Boswell-Wilkie Circus v. Brian Boswell Circus* [1986] F.S.R. 479.

8. THE RELIEF GRANTED

16–97 **Form of injunction**

NEW ILLUSTRATION 3. The plaintiff established that it had traded under "Chelsea Man" in Coventry, Leicester and the area of Oxford Street in London. The defendants argued that the plaintiff's reputation was limited to these areas and that any injunction should be limited accordingly. At first instance the judge, whilst not finding that the plaintiff had a nationwide reputation, expressly rejected the contention that reputation was limited to the three areas. On appeal, applying *Ewing v. Buttercup Margarine* [1917] 2 Ch. 1 and *Brestian v. Try* [1958] R.P.C. 161, the Court of Appeal held that an injunction could extend beyond the particular areas where reputation and goodwill had been proved. Since the defendant's intended use of the name was nationwide, a nationwide injunction was appropriate: *Chelsea Man v. Chelsea Girl* [1987] R.P.C. 189 (C.A.).

Qualified injunctions

16–98

A disclaimer is not appropriate where it is unlikely to come to the attention of the reader and may well confuse him further if it does: *Associated Newspapers v. Insert Media* [1991] F.S.R. 380 (C.A.).

Passing-off abroad

16–101

The plaintiff failed to establish even an arguable case in passing-off in circumstances where all that had happened in the United Kingdom was the receipt of letters and cheques from persons to whom misrepresentations were made outside the United Kingdom: *Intercontext v. Schmidt* [1988] F.S.R. 575. In addition, applying *Alfred Dunhill v. Sunoptic* [1979] F.S.R. 337, where the plaintiff alleged that passing-off abroad was actionable in the United Kingdom, it was not sufficient to rely on the presumption that foreign law was the same as English law. Evidence of the relevant foreign law must be provided.

See also *L.A. Gear v. Gerald Whelan* [1991] F.S.R. 670, *ante*, para. 14–13.

Interim injunctions

16–102

See also the Main Work, §§ 15–65 and 15–66, and *ante*, para. 15–65.

General

It has been emphasised by the Court of Appeal that the *American Cyanamid* principles apply to passing-off actions: *County Sound v. Ocean Sound* [1991] F.S.R. 367, *ante*, para. 16–12. At the same time, the Court expressed a robust view that in some cases the judge hearing the interlocutory application can see at once that there is no serious question to be tried as to confusion, and in others that there is no real possibility that a defence will succeed at trial.

For a more recent case where the judge concluded that the plaintiffs had failed to establish a serious issue to be determined at trial both in relation to an allegation of passing-off and injurious falsehood, see *Ciba Geigy v. Parke Davis* [1994] F.S.R. 8.

If the plaintiff has established an arguable case but the merits are not clear, then the *Cyanamid* principles apply.

Will damages be an adequate remedy for the plaintiff?

Where the plaintiff has established an arguable case, it is likely that damages will not be an adequate remedy because of the difficulty of establishing the extent of confusion and damage and of quantifying it in monetary terms. For a recent case see, for example, *Morgan Grampian v. Training Personnel* [1992] F.S.R. 267.

The risk of a plaintiff suffering a swamping of his reputation by a larger defendant is something which is often claimed but rarely made out on the evidence. For a case where swamping was a real risk and a material factor in the balance of convenience, see *Provident Financial v. Halifax Building Society* [1994] F.S.R. 81.

Will damages be an adequate remedy for the defendant?

Where the defendant has started to use the mark in issue, then damages will not usually be an adequate remedy. The defendant will have to adopt a new mark with consequential delay and, perhaps, embarrassment in the trade and amongst the public. If the defendant has committed nothing apart from money to its new mark and the plaintiff is in a position to pay, then it is possible that damages would be an adequate remedy. But even here the defendant may argue that it is being deprived of the name of choice and that this may have an effect on trade. Further once a new name has been chosen it may never be possible to revert to the name of choice.

Balance of justice

On the assumption that damages would not be an adequate remedy to either side, the court must consider the balance of convenience generally, which is now recognised as choosing the course which appears to involve the least risk of causing injustice. See, *e.g. Management Publications v. Blenheim Group* [1991] F.S.R. 348 and 550 (C.A.). See also *Cayne v. Global Natural Resources* [1984] 1 All E.R. 225.

It may be that the damage which one party is likely to suffer is more easily quantifiable and ascertainable than any damage which the other may suffer. The extent of any damage which may be suffered, how likely it is to be suffered and whether it would be irreparable are all factors which are commonly taken into account. The ability of each party to pay may be particularly relevant.

In recent cases the following matters have received particular consideration.

Factors which may favour the plaintiff

Confusion may not come to light and dilution of and damage to goodwill are very difficult to quantify: *Morgan Grampian v. Training Personnel* [1992] F.S.R. 267; *Taittinger v. Allbev* [1992] F.S.R. 647.

The balance may favour a plaintiff where there is a real risk of confusion and damage to the plaintiff, and the defendant can adopt another name or continue with what it was doing before. See, for example, *Morgan Grampian v. Training Personnel* [1992] F.S.R. 267; *Taittinger v. Allbev* [1992] F.S.R. 647.

So also where the defendant has shown a lack of prudence and care in the choice of its new name in failing to check whether that name was being used by another: *Morgan Grampian v. Training Personnel* [1992] F.S.R. 267.

Factors which may favour the defendant

Although the court is unable to come to a clear conclusion on the merits it may nevertheless be necessary to consider the risk of persons being misled pending a further hearing or trial. See *Financial Times v. Evening Standard* [1991] F.S.R. 7; *Management Publications v. Blenheim Exhibitions Group* [1991] F.S.R. 348 and 550 (C.A.).

For cases where the risk of deception was not great and the consequences to the plaintiff were unlikely to be severe, see *Stacey v. 2020 Communications* [1991] F.S.R. 49; *Management Publications v. Blenheim Group* [1991] F.S.R. 348 and 550 (C.A.).

However, to assess the risk of confusion is not the right approach where it entails a "not-so-mini" trial on affidavit evidence of an issue of fact which is in dispute. Nevertheless, it may be appropriate to consider what the consequences of any confusion pending trial would be: *Blazer v. Yardley* [1992] F.S.R. 501. Thus, though it was possible that substantial numbers of persons would make the association between the defendant's products and the plaintiff's, the risk of damage pending trial was not sufficient to outweigh the damage that would be caused to the defendant; (the mark was proposed to be used as an international brand).

It may be very material on the balance of convenience if the grant of an injunction would probably result in the defendant having to abandon its chosen name permanently: *Boots v. Approved Prescription Services* [1988] F.S.R. 45; *Post Office v. Interlink* [1989] F.S.R. 369; *Stacey v. 2020 Communications* [1991] F.S.R. 49; *Gala of London v. Chandler* [1991] F.S.R. 294; *Management Publications v. Blenheim Exhibitions Group* [1991] F.S.R. 348 and 550 (C.A.); *Blazer v. Yardley* [1992] F.S.R. 501; see also the Main Work, § 15–66, note 84.

Delay or lack of activity may also provide some indication of whether the plaintiff is genuinely concerned to preserve its assets by due process of law: *Gala of London v. Chandler* [1991] F.S.R. 294.

Other factors

In *Nationwide Building Society v. Nationwide Estate Agents* [1987] F.S.R. 579, the judge was prepared to grant an interlocutory injunction, but for one factor. At the initial hearing of the motion the defendants had undertaken not to expand their use of "Nationwide". Whilst the defendants were tied to the starting post, the plaintiff had gone ahead as fast as possible to establish its own estate agency business. The court declined to allow its jurisdiction to be used to obtain an unfair commercial advantage, unless both parties kept out of the market until trial.

Status quo

The status quo is the state of affairs existing immediately preceding the issue of the writ or, if there be unreasonable delay between the issue of the writ and the motion for an interlocutory injunction, the period immediately preceding the motion: *Garden Cottage Foods v. Milk Marketing Board* [1984] A.C. 130.

Footnote 33: The relevance of freedom of speech. See also *Microdata v. Rivendale* (C.A.) September 11, 1984, now reported [1991] F.S.R. 681, a case based on unlawful interference with contractual relations. The mere fact that an action could have been framed in defamation is not of itself a sufficient justification for applying the principle in defamation proceedings that no interlocutory injunction will be granted. May L.J. expressed the opinion (at 686) that the principle ought not to be extended further than is necessary in order to preserve the fundamental right of free speech. Griffiths L.J. considered (at 688) that in such a case the court weighs in the balance the right of free speech against the right asserted by the plaintiff in his alternative cause of action. *Microdata* has been followed in *Western Front v. Vestron* [1987] F.S.R. 66.

Consorzio del Prosciutto di Parma v. Marks & Spencer ("Parma Ham") [1990] F.S.R. 530. In this case the question of interference with freedom of speech was considered under the heading of balance of convenience. On appeal ([1991] R.P.C. 351) the whole claim was struck out and accordingly the issue did not arise.

Essex Electric (PTE.) v. IPC Computers [1991] F.S.R. 690. The plaintiffs obtained an injunction to restrain an alleged abuse of process and unlawful interference with contract where the claims included an allegation of trade libel.

Compaq Computer v. Dell Computer [1992] F.S.R. 93, *post*, para. 18–20.

16–105 Innocent defendant

Footnote 41A: *McDonalds v. Burger King* is now reported at [1987] F.S.R. 112.

9. Practice

16–107 Generally

See *Colgate-Palmolive v. Markwell Finance* [1990] R.P.C. 197, *ante*, para. 15–89.

DECEPTIVE RESEMBLANCE

3. RULES OF COMPARISON

(a) The "Idea of the Mark" is to be regarded   **17–08**

"Porta", for portable buildings, held to be infringed by "Portoblast". The first five letters of "Portoblast" and "Porta" looked alike and sounded alike. The addition of the letters "blast" did not diminish the resemblance, but rather was likely to suggest that the product was an addition to the range of the plaintiff's products which had long been identified in various forms by using, as part of the mark, "Porta". *Portakabin v. Powerblast* [1990] R.P.C. 471. (See also *post*, paras. 17–21 and 17–29.)

NEW ILLUSTRATION 15. The plaintiff's mark comprised an oval border,   **17–09** which enclosed "Laura Ashley", and a botanical sprig. The defendant's mark comprised a similar oval border, enclosing "Coloroll", and a different sprig. The plaintiff contended that the essential feature of the mark was the oval border. Whitford J. disagreed. His initial view was that the essential feature was "Laura Ashley" and the evidence did not persuade him from that view: *Laura Ashley v. Coloroll* [1987] R.P.C. 1.

Ear as well as eye must be considered   **17–15**

In a case where "Treat Size" was not used as a trade mark and did not infringe upon "Treets", Whitford J. observed that the sound of a mark was diminishing in importance when brand names appear clearly on packaging and goods are available on self-service displays: *Mars v. Cadbury* [1987] R.P.C. 387.

FOOTNOTE 66:   In *"Star"* [1990] R.P.C. 522 (Regy.), "Star" was considered too close to "Spar" both visually and phonetically for food products.

FOOTNOTE 69:   In *"Lancer"* [1987] R.P.C. 303, "Lancer" was considered not too close to "Lancia" since the connotations of the two marks were different; the purchase of a car was not an everyday purchase over the counter and alleged confusion caused by mishearing at a cocktail party was fanciful.

(d) Marks are to be compared as they would be seen in actual use   **17–17**

In *Levi Strauss v. Kimbyr Investments* (Williams J., High Court of New Zealand, June 28, 1993 [1994] F.S.R. 335) the Judge accepted that it was legitimate and classic use of a mark to maintain the connection between the goods and the proprietor of the mark during the life of the goods *after* sale, particularly where the occasional repeat order business was "of exceptional importance".

In that case Levi Strauss succeeded in proving infringement of their "tab" mark in respect of jeans. Much of the evidence of confusion related to "post-sale" confusion, in that witnesses considered jeans as they would appear being worn after sale. At the point of sale, cardboard labels and the like were sufficient to eliminate confusion unless the purchaser took only a cursory glance at the labels. After sale, those labels were removed, leaving the tab in the seam of a rear pocket of the jeans.

FOOTNOTE 76: See *Laura Ashley v. Coloroll* [1987] R.P.C. 1 at 11, where the judge expressly disapproved of so-called T-scope tests (see *post*, para. 17–28, n. 11), observing (following *"June"*) that trade marks have to be considered in a business context and not in the context of laboratory experiments.

17–21   (e) All the circumstances of the trade to be considered

See *Portakabin v. Powerblast* [1990] R.P.C. 471, *ante*, para. 17–08 and *post*, para. 17–29. Amongst the circumstances taken into account were that the range of potential customers for the plaintiffs' portable buildings was wide enough to include customers for the defendant's "Portablast" shot blasting units and that the plaintiffs' products covered the widest kind of use.

It may be proper to take into account that goods are sometimes purchased for others and that the customer may not know the purpose for which the goods are required: *"Inadine"* [1992] R.P.C. 421.

17–23   Numerous marks of the same kind on the Register

FOOTNOTE 98:   And see *"Terbuline"* [1990] R.P.C. 21 (B.o.T.).

4. EVIDENCE

17–25   Evidence as to probability of deception

The first sentence of this paragraph of the Main Work was expressly approved by Dillon L.J. in *Mothercare v. Penguin Books* [1988] R.P.C. 113 at 116, and referred to by Knox J. in *Island Trading v. Anchor Brewing* [1989] R.P.C. 287a.

17–27   Expert evidence

In the course of the trial in *"Jif"*, the evidence of a market researcher called to give evidence of "image tracking studies", designed to test for brand awareness, was held not to be expert evidence. He was giving evidence of the summation of his results, not as to his opinion of anything: *Reckitt &*

Colman v. Borden [1987] F.S.R. 407.

In an area which requires specialised knowledge – such as the habits of designer label buyers – it is permissible for trade witnesses to give evidence as to the likely reactions and behaviour of their customers and whether those customers would be confused: *Guccio Gucci v. Paulo Gucci* [1991] F.S.R. 89.

Direct evidence of probability of deception   17–28

Surveys

In *Scott v. Nice-Pak* [1989] F.S.R. 100, the survey relied upon by the plaintiff was held so flawed it could not be relied upon. There were two main vices. Some questions were leading, some proceeded on a false basis and some questions suffered from both vices. Two examples:

1. False basis: interviewees were shown one of the defendant's blue tubs of baby wipes and asked "Have you ever seen or bought this make of baby wipe?", when the defendant's tubs had not been marketed or available for sale in the United Kingdom.
2. Both vices: an interviewee was asked, "Why do you think that you mistook baby wipes for 'Baby Fresh' [the plaintiff's baby wipes in a blue tub]?", where the interviewee had not said she was mistaken.

Surveys were used to effect in *Reckitt & Colman v. Borden ("Jif")* [1990] R.P.C. 341 (H.L.), a *quia timet* action. The surveys conducted are summarised at 350.

In *United Biscuits v. Burtons Biscuits* [1992] F.S.R. 14, the surveys were found to be of no value.

In *Levi Strauss v. Kimbyr Investments* (Williams J., High Court of New Zealand, June 28, 1993 [1994] F.S.R. 335), infringement of the plaintiff's "tab" mark for jeans was found, partly on the basis of a survey in which the participants were shown a stylised drawing of a pair of jeans in which the tab was shown as positioned on the infringing jeans (on the right-hand side of a rear pocket) whereas Levi Strauss put their tab on the left hand seam of the right rear pocket.

Footnote 11:   *Laura Ashley v. Coloroll* now reported at [1987] R.P.C. 1.

Footnote 14:   But see *Guccio Gucci v. Paulo Gucci* [1991] F.S.R. 89, *ante*, para. 17–27.

Footnote 16:   In *Island Trading v. Anchor Brewing* [1989] R.P.C. 287a, Knox J. said that the passage at 468 of *"Sodastream"* must be read in its context, there being no issue in that case of admissibility. Applying *Ballantine v. Ballantyne Stewart* [1959] R.P.C. 273 at 280, Knox J. admitted statements that the public identified the plaintiff's product as "Steam beer" and ordered it as such, and also evidence from publicans concerning their policy in the light of what they regarded as likely customer reaction. Direct statements of opinion by deponents that it was possible or probable that the public would be confused were held inadmissible.

17–29   Evidence of actual deception

FOOTNOTE 28:   See *Portakabin v. Powerblast* [1990] R.P.C. 471, *ante*, paras. 17–08 and 17–21. It was not surprising that there was no evidence of actual confusion, in view of the specialised nature of the equipment produced by the defendant, the relatively low number of sales and the paucity of promotional material using the defendant's mark.

17–30   Intention to deceive need not be proved

This paragraph was referred to with approval by Williams J. in *Levi Strauss v. Kimbyr Investments* (High Court of New Zealand, June 28, 1993 [1994] F.S.R. 335) where the Judge made the finding that there was no satisfactory explanation for the defendant's adoption of a "tab" mark on jeans other than to capitalise on the plaintiff's goodwill.

CHAPTER 18

TRADE LIBEL

1. THREATS

18–05   A warning against infringements, etc., may be issued in good faith

It may be appropriate to require a defendant to disclose before trial the names and addresses of all persons to whom the allegedly malicious statements have been made so that the plaintiff can mitigate its loss by disabusing them of any false impression: *CHC Software Care v. Hopkins & Wood* [1993] F.S.R. 241.

2. TRADE LIBEL GENERALLY

18–06   FOOTNOTE 17:   For a recent restatement of the essentials of the tort, see *Kaye v. Robertson* [1991] F.S.R. 62 (C.A.). The plaintiff, an actor, was recovering in hospital from a serious accident and was in no condition to be interviewed or to give any informed consent to be interviewed. The defendants gained access to his room, interviewed and photographed him, and proposed to publish an article in the *Sunday Sport* saying he had consented to be interviewed and describing the article as exclusive. An interim injunction to restrain malicious falsehood was granted. A further claim of libel, in that the article would have the effect of lowering the plaintiff in the esteem of right thinking people, was held to be arguable, but no injunction was granted on the basis of the usual rule in actions for defamation.

Proof of damage (Defamation Act 1952)   18–08

The loss of a potentially valuable opportunity to sell a story to a journal would constitute damage sufficient to maintain the cause of action: *Kaye v. Robertson* [1991] F.S.R. 62 (C.A.), *ante*, para. 18–06.

Meaning of "malice"   18–09

Malice will be inferred if it be proved that the words were calculated to produce damage and that the defendant knew when he published the words that they were false, or was reckless as to whether they were false or not: *Kaye v. Robertson* [1991] F.S.R. 62 (C.A.), *ante*, para. 18–06.

3. PROCEEDINGS

Interlocutory injunction   18–20

See also *ante*, para. 16–102.

Where statements have been made which cannot be justified, then an interlocutory injunction may be granted if the balance of justice is in favour of so doing.

Thus, in *Kaye v. Robertson* [1991] F.S.R. 62 at 66 (C.A.), *ante*, para. 18–06, an interim injunction was granted to restrain the defendants from:

> "publishing causing to be published or permitting to be published anything which could be reasonably understood or convey to any person reading or looking at the Defendants' *Sunday Sport* newspaper that the Plaintiff had voluntarily permitted any photographs to be taken for publication in that newspaper or had voluntarily permitted representatives of the Defendants to interview him while a patient in the Charing Cross hospital undergoing treatment".

No injunction was granted in respect of the alleged defamation.

Where there is a dispute as to whether a representation has been made but no dispute that if it has been made then it cannot be justified, then the correct approach is to apply the *Cyanamid* rules; and when considering the balance of justice it is right to consider the question of freedom of speech. See *Compaq Computer v. Dell Computer* [1992] F.S.R. 93 in which the defendants published a series of advertisements comparing their computer systems to those of the plaintiffs as to price and quality. The plaintiffs complained that the comparisons contained false representations in that they were unfair and misleading in a number of respects. The defendants argued, *inter alia*, that the representations were not made. Held, granting an interim injunction, the defendants could change their advertisements so as to continue making a comparison but without using the elements said to constitute false representations.

CHAPTER 19

REGISTRATION OF FOREIGN TRADE MARKS

2. COMMONWEALTH AND FOREIGN TRADE MARKS

19–22   Registration of trade mark by importer

See also "*Sabatier*" [1993] R.P.C. 97 (Regy.), *ante*, para. 2–21.

CHAPTER 20

MISCELLANEOUS MATTERS

1. FALSE REPRESENTATIONS

20–01   False representation as to registration of trade marks

See also *ante*, para. 15–54.

Miscellaneous Matters

2. Allowance of Income Tax in Respect of Registration of Trade Marks

Section 132 of the Income and Corporation Taxes Act 1970 was repealed **20–07** by the Income and Corporation Taxes Act 1988, Schedule 31. The equivalent provision is now contained in section 83 of the Income and Corporation Taxes Act 1988 as amended by the Copyright, Designs and Patents Act 1988, section 303(1), Schedule 7, paragraph 36.

5. Plant Variety Names

Footnote 25:   See now Plant Breeders' Rights Regulations 1978 (S.I. 1978 **20–10** No. 294) as amended.

6. Company and Business Names

Note that section 691 of the Companies Act 1985 was amended by the **20–13** Companies Act 1989, section 145, Schedule 19, paragraph 6.

APPENDICES

TRADE MARKS ACT 1938

ARRANGEMENT OF SECTIONS

Offences and restraint of use of Royal Arms

A1–00T/
A1–00S

New sections 58A to 58D have been added to the 1938 Act after the heading of   **A1–59T**
"*Offences and restraint of Royal Arms*" by section 300 of the Copyright, Designs and
Patents Act 1988 as follows, with effect from August 1, 1989:

Fraudulent application or use of trade mark an offence   **A1–58A**

58A.—(1) It is an offence, subject to subsection (3) below, for a person—
(a) to apply a mark identical to or nearly resembling a registered trade mark to
    goods, or to material used or intended to be used for labelling, packaging or
    advertising goods, or
(b) to sell, let for hire, or offer or expose for sale or hire, or distribute—
    (i) goods bearing such a mark, or
    (ii) material bearing such a mark which is used or intended to be used for
         labelling, packaging or advertising goods, or
(c) to use material bearing such a mark in the course of a business for labelling,
    packaging or advertising goods, or
(d) to possess in the course of a business goods or material bearing such a mark
        with a view to doing any of the things mentioned in paragraphs (a) to (c),
when he is not entitled to use the mark in relation to the goods in question and the
goods are not connected in the course of trade with a person who is so entitled.

(2) It is also an offence, subject to subsection (3) below, for a person to possess in
the course of a business goods or material bearing a mark identical to or nearly
resembling a registered trade mark with a view to enabling or assisting another
person to do any of the things mentioned in subsection (1)(a) to (c), knowing or
having reason to believe that the other person is not entitled to use the mark in
relation to the goods in question and that the goods are not connected in the course of
trade with a person who is so entitled.

(3) A person commits an offence under subsection (1) or (2) only if—
(a) he acts with a view to gain for himself or another, or with intent to cause loss to
    another, and
(b) he intends that the goods in question should be accepted as connected in the
        course of trade with a person entitled to use the mark in question;
and it is a defence for a person charged with an offence under subsection (1) to show

67

that he believed on reasonable grounds that he was entitled to use the mark in relation to the goods in question.

(4) A person guilty of an offence under this section is liable—

(a) on summary conviction to imprisonment for a term not exceeding six months or a fine not exceeding the statutory maximum, or both;

(b) on conviction on indictment to a fine or imprisonment for a term not exceeding ten years, or both.

(5) Where an offence under this section committed by a body corporate is proved to have been committed with the consent or connivance of a director, manager, secretary or other similar officer of the body, or a person purporting to act in any such capacity, he as well as the body corporate is guilty of the offence and liable to be proceeded against and punished accordingly.

In relation to a body corporate whose affairs are managed by its members "director" means a member of the body corporate.

(6) In this section "business" includes a trade or profession.

A1–58B   **Delivery of offending goods and material**

58B.—(1) The court by which a person is convicted of an offence under section 58A may, if satisfied that at the time of his arrest or charge he had in his possession, custody or control—

(a) goods or material in respect of which the offence was committed, or

(b) goods of the same description as those in respect of which the offence was committed, or material similar to that in respect of which the offence was committed, bearing a mark identical to or nearly resembling that in relation to which the offence was committed,

order that the goods or material be delivered up to such person as the court may direct.

(2) For this purpose a person shall be treated as charged with an offence—

(a) in England, Wales and Northern Ireland, when he is orally charged or is served with a summons or indictment;

(b) in Scotland, when he is cautioned, charged or served with a complaint or indictment.

(3) An order may be made by the court of its own motion or on the application of the prosecutor (or, in Scotland, the Lord Advocate or procurator-fiscal), but shall not be made if it appears to the court unlikely that any order will be made under section 58C (order as to disposal of offending goods or material).

(4) An appeal lies from an order made under this section by a magistrates' court—

(a) in England and Wales, to the Crown Court, and

(b) in Northern Ireland, to the county court;

and in Scotland, where an order has been made under this section, the person from whose possession, custody or control the goods or material have been removed may, without prejudice to any other form of appeal under any rule of law, appeal against that order in the same manner as against sentence.

(5) A person to whom goods or material are delivered up in pursuance of an order under this section shall retain it pending the making of an order under section 58C.

(6) Nothing in this section affects the powers of the court under section 43 of the Powers of Criminal Courts Act 1973, section 223 or 436 of the Criminal Procedure (Scotland) Act 1975 or Article 7 of the Criminal Justice (Northern Ireland) Order 1980 (general provisions as to forfeiture in criminal proceedings).

Order as to disposal of offending goods or material   A1–58C

58C.—(1) Where goods or material have been delivered up in pursuance of an order under section 58B, an application may be made to the court for an order that they be destroyed or forfeited to such person as the court may think fit.

(2) Provision shall be made by rules of court as to the service of notice on persons having an interest in the goods or material, and any such person is entitled—
   (a) to appear in proceedings for an order under this section, whether or not he was served with notice, and
   (b) to appeal against any order made, whether or not he appeared;
and an order shall not take effect until the end of the period within which notice of an appeal may be given or, if before the end of that period notice of appeal is duly given, until the final determination or abandonment of the proceedings on the appeal.

(3) Where there is more than one person interested in goods or material, the court shall make such order as it thinks just.

(4) References in this section to a person having an interest in goods or material include any person in whose favour an order could be made under this section or under sections 114, 204 or 231 of the Copyright, Designs and Patents Act 1988 (which make similar provision in relation to infringement of copyright, rights in performances and design right).

(5) Proceedings for an order under this section may be brought—
   (a) in a county court in England, Wales and Northern Ireland, provided the value of the goods or material in question does not exceed the county court limit for actions in tort, and
   (b) in a sheriff court in Scotland;
but this shall not be construed as affecting the jurisdiction of the High Court or, in Scotland, the Court of Session.

Enforcement of section 58A   A1–58D

58D.—(1) The functions of a local weights and measures authority include the enforcement in their area of section 58A.

(2) The following provisions of the Trade Descriptions Act 1968 apply in relation to the enforcement of that section as in relation to the enforcement of that Act—
   section 27 (power to make test purchases),
   section 28 (power to enter premises and inspect and seize goods and documents),
   section 29 (obstruction of authorised officers), and
   section 33 (compensation for loss, &c. of goods seized under s.28).

(3) Subsection (1) above does not apply in relation to the enforcement of section 58A in Northern Ireland, but the functions of the Department of Economic Development include the enforcement of that section in Northern Ireland.

For that purpose the provisions of the Trade Descriptions Act 1968 specified in subsection (2) apply as if for the references to a local weights and measures authority and any officer of such an authority there were substituted references to that Department and any of its officers.

(4) Any enactment which authorises the disclosure of information for the purpose of facilitating the enforcement of the Trade Descriptions Act 1968 shall apply as if section 58A above were contained in that Act and as if the functions of any person in relation to the enforcement of that section were functions under that Act.

Appendix 1A

FIRST COUNCIL DIRECTIVE

of December 21, 1988
to approximate the laws of the Member States relating to trade marks

(89/104/EEC: [1989] O.J. L40/1)

The Council of the European Communities

A1A–01 Having regard to the Treaty establishing the European Economic Community, and in particular Article 110a thereof,
Having regard to the proposal from the Commission,
In cooperation with the European Parliament,
Having regard to the opinion of the Economic and Social Committee,
(1) Whereas[1] the trade mark laws at present applicable in the Member States contain disparities which may impede the free movement of goods and freedom to provide services and may distort competition within the common market; whereas it is therefore necessary, in view of the establishment and functioning of the internal market, to approximate the laws of Member States;
(2) Whereas it is important not to disregard the solutions and advantages which the Community trade mark system may afford to undertakings wishing to acquire trade marks;
(3) Whereas it does not appear to be necessary at present to undertake full-scale approximation of the trade mark laws of the Member States and it will be sufficient if approximation is limited to those national provisions of law which most directly affect the functioning of the internal market;
(4) Whereas the Directive does not deprive the Member States of the right to continue to protect trade marks acquired through use but takes them into account only in regard to the relationship between them and trade marks acquired by registration;
(5) Whereas Member States also remain free to fix the provisions of procedure concerning the registration, the revocation and the invalidity of trade marks acquired by registration; whereas they can, for example, determine the form of trade mark registration and invalidity procedures, decide whether earlier rights should be invoked either in the registration procedure or in the invalidity procedure or in both

---

[1] Recitals numbered editorially.

and, if they allow earlier rights to be invoked in the registration procedure, have an opposition procedure or an *ex officio* examination procedure or both; whereas Member States remain free to determine the effects of revocation or invalidity of trade marks;

(6) Whereas this Directive does not exclude the application to trade marks of provisions of law of the Member States other than trade mark law, such as the provisions relating to unfair competition, civil liability or consumer protection;

(7) Whereas attainment of the objectives at which this approximation of laws is aiming requires that the conditions for obtaining and continuing to hold a registered trade mark are, in general, identical in all Member States; whereas, to this end, it is necessary to list examples of signs which may constitute a trade mark, provided that such signs are capable of distinguishing the goods or services of one undertaking from those of other undertakings; whereas the grounds for refusal or invalidity concerning the trade mark itself, for example, the absence of any distinctive character, or concerning conflicts between the trade mark and earlier rights, are to be listed in an exhaustive manner, even if some of these grounds are listed as an option for the Member States which will therefore be able to maintain or introduce those grounds in their legislation; whereas Member States will be able to maintain or introduce into their legislation grounds of refusal or invalidity linked to conditions for obtaining and continuing to hold a trade mark for which there is no provision of approximation, concerning, for example, the eligibility for the grant of a trade mark, the renewal of the trade mark or rules on fees, or related to the non-compliance with procedural rules;

(8) Whereas in order to reduce the total number of trade marks registered and protected in the Community and, consequently, the number of conflicts which arise between them, it is essential to require that registered trade marks must actually be used or, if not used, be subject to revocation; whereas it is necessary to provide that a trade mark cannot be invalidated on the basis of the exitence of a non-used earlier trade mark, while the Member States remain free to apply the same principle in respect of the registration of a trade mark or to provide that a trade mark may not be successfully invoked in infringement proceedings if it is established as a result of a plea that the trade mark could be revoked; whereas in all these cases it is up to the Member States to establish the applicable rules of procedure; **A1A–02**

(9) Whereas it is fundamental, in order to facilitate the free circulation of goods and services, to ensure that henceforth registered trade marks enjoy the same protection under the legal systems of all the Member States; whereas this should however not prevent the Member States from granting at their option extensive protection to those trade marks which have a reputation;

(10) Whereas the protection afforded by the registered trade mark, the function of which is in particular to guarantee the trade mark as an indication of origin, is absolute in the case of identity between the mark and the sign and goods or services; whereas the protection applies also in case of similarity between the mark and the sign and the goods or services; whereas it is indispensable to give an interpretation of the concept of similarity in relation to the likelihood of confusion; whereas the likelihood of confusion, the appreciation of which depends on numerous elements and, in particular, on the recognition of the trade mark on the market, of the association which can be made with the used or registered sign, of the degree of similarity between the trade mark and the sign and between the goods or services identified, constitutes the specific condition for such protection; whereas the ways in which likelihood of confusion may be established, and in particular the onus of proof, are a matter for national procedural rules which are not prejudiced by the Directive;

(11) Whereas it is important, for reasons of legal certainty and without inequitably

prejudicing the interests of a proprietor of an earlier trade mark, to provide that the latter may no longer request a declaration of invalidity nor may he oppose the use of a trade mark subsequent to his own of which he has knowingly tolerated the use for a substantial length of time, unless the application for the subsequent trade mark was made in bad faith;

(12) Whereas all Member States of the Community are bound by the Paris Convention for the Protection of Industrial Property; whereas it is necessary that the provisions of this Directive are entirely consistent with those of the Paris Convention; whereas the obligations of the Member States resulting from this Convention are not affected by this Directive; whereas, where appropriate, the second sub-paragraph of Article 234 of the Treaty is applicable,

HAS ADOPTED THIS DIRECTIVE:

A1A–03

Article 1

Scope

This Directive shall apply to every trade mark in respect of goods or services which is the subject of registration or of an application in a Member State for registration as an individual trade mark, a collective mark or a guarantee or certification mark, or which is the subject of a registration or an application for registration in the Benelux Trade Mark Office or of an international registration having effect in a Member State.

A1A–04

Article 2

Signs of which a trade mark may consist

A trade mark may consist of any sign capable of being represented graphically, particularly words, including personal names, designs, letters, numerals, the shape of goods or of their packaging, provided that such signs are capable of distinguishing the goods or services of one undertaking from those of other undertakings.

A1A–05

Article 3

Grounds for refusal or invalidity

1. The following shall not be registered or if registered shall be liable to be declared invalid:
    (a) signs which cannot constitute a trade mark;
    (b) trade marks which are devoid of any distinctive character;
    (c) trade marks which consist exclusively of signs or indications which may serve, in trade, to designate the kind, quality, quantity, intended purpose, value, geographical origin, or the time of production of the goods or of rendering of the service, or other characteristics of the goods or service;
    (d) trade marks which consist exclusively of signs or indications which have become customary in the current language or in the bona fide and established practices of the trade;
    (e) signs which consist exclusively of:
    — the shape which results from the nature of the goods themselves, or
    — the shape of goods which is necessary to obtain a technical result, or
    — the shape which gives substantial value to the goods;

    (f) trade marks which are contrary to public policy or to accepted principles of morality;

    (g) trade marks which are of such a nature as to deceive the public, for instance as to the nature, quality or geographical origin of the goods or service;

    (h) trade marks which have not been authorized by the competent authorities and are to be refused or invalidated pursuant to Article 6 *ter* of the Paris Convention for the Protection of Industrial Property, hereinafter referred to as the 'Paris Convention'.

2.   Any Member State may provide that a trade mark shall not be registered or, if registered, shall be liable to be declared invalid where and to the extent that:

    (a) the use of that trade mark may be prohibited pursuant to provisions of law other than trade mark law of the Member State concerned or of the Community;

    (b) the trade mark covers a sign of high symbolic value, in particular a religious symbol;

    (c) the trade mark includes badges, emblems and escutcheons other than those covered by Article 6 *ter* of the Paris Convention and which are of public interest, unless the consent of the appropriate authorities to its registration has been given in conformity with the legislation of the Member State;

    (d) the application for registration of the trade mark was made in bad faith by the applicant.

3.   A trade mark shall not be refused registration or be declared invalid in accordance with paragraph 1(b), (c) or (d) if, before the date of application for registration and following the use which has been made of it, it has acquired a distinctive character. Any Member State may in addition provide that this provision shall also apply where the distinctive character was acquired after the date of application for registration or after the date of registration.

4.   Any Member State may provide that, by derogation from the preceding paragraphs, the grounds of refusal of registration or invalidity in force in that State prior to the date on which the provisions necessary to comply with this Directive enter into force, shall apply to trade marks for which application has been made prior to that date.

Article 4   **A1A–06**

Further grounds for refusal or invalidity concerning conflicts with earlier rights

1.   A trade mark shall not be registered or, if registered, shall be liable to be declared invalid:

    (a) if it is identical with an earlier trade mark, and the goods or services for which the trade mark is applied for or is registered are identical with the goods or services for which the earlier trade mark is protected;

    (b) if because of its identity with, or similarity to, the earlier trade mark and the identity or similarity of the goods or services covered by the trade marks, there exists a likelihood of confusion on the part of the public, which includes the likelihood of association with the earlier trade mark.

2.   "Earlier trade marks" within the meaning of paragraph 1 means:

    (a) trade marks of the following kinds with a date of application for registration which is earlier than the date of application for registration of the trade mark, taking account, where appropriate, of the priorities claimed in respect of those trade marks;

      (i) Community trade marks;

      (ii) trade marks registered in the Member State or, in the case of Belgium,

Luxembourg or the Netherlands, at the Benelux Trade Mark Office;

    (iii) trade marks registered under international arrangements which have effect in the Member State;

(b) Community trade marks which validly claim seniority, in accordance with the Regulation on the Community trade mark, from a trade mark referred to in (a)(ii) and (iii), even when the latter trade mark has been surrendered or allowed to lapse;

(c) applications for the trade marks referred to in (a) and (b), subject to their registration;

(d) trade marks which, on the date of application for registration of the trade mark or, where appropriate, of the priority claimed in respect of the application for registration of the trade mark, are well known in a Member State, in the sense in which the words "well known" are used in Article 6 *bis* of the Paris Convention;

3. A trade mark shall furthermore not be registered or, if registered, shall be liable to be declared invalid if it is identical with, or similar to, an earlier Community trade mark within the meaning of paragraph 2 and is to be, or has been, registered for goods or services which are not similar to those for which the earlier Community trade mark is registered, where the earlier Community trade mark as a reputation in the Community and where the use of the later trade mark without due cause would take unfair advantage of, or be detrimental to, the distinctive character or the repute of the earlier Community trade mark.

4. Any Member State may furthermore provide that a trade mark shall not be registered or, if registered, shall be liable to be declared invalid where, and to the extent that:

(a) the trade mark is identical with, or similar to, an earlier national trade mark within the meaning of paragraph 2 and is to be, or has been, registered for goods or services which are not similar to those for which the earlier trade mark is registered, where the earlier trade mark has a reputation in the Member State concerned and where the use of the later trade mark without due cause would take unfair advantage of, or be detrimental to, the distinctive character or the repute of the earlier trade mark;

(b) rights to a non-registered trade mark or to another sign used in the course of trade were acquired prior to the date of application for registration of the subsequent trade mark, or the date of the priority claimed for the application for registration of the subsequent trade mark and that non-registered trade mark or other sign confers on its proprietor the right to prohibit the use of a subsequent trade mark;

(c) the use of the trade mark may be prohibited by virtue of an earlier right other than the rights referred to in paragraphs 2 and 4(b) and in particular:

    (i) a right to a name;

    (ii) a right of personal portrayal;

    (iii) a copyright;

    (iv) an industrial property right;

(d) the trade mark is identical with, or similar to, an earlier collective trade mark conferring a right which expired within a period of a maximum of three years preceding application;

(e) the trade mark is identical with, or similar to, an earlier guarantee or certification mark conferring a right which expired within a period preceding application the length of which is fixed by the Member State;

(f) the trade mark is identical with, or similar to, an earlier trade mark which was registered for identical or similar goods or services and conferred on them a right which has expired for failure to renew within a period of a maximum of two years preceding application, unless the proprietor of the earlier trade mark gave his agreement for the registration of the later mark or did not use his trade mark;

(g) the trade mark is liable to be confused with a mark which was in use abroad on the filing date of the application and which is still in use there, provided that at the date of the application the applicant was acting in bad faith.

5. The Member States may permit that in appropriate circumstances registration need not be refused or the trade mark need not be declared invalid where the proprietor of the earlier trade mark or other earlier right consents to the registration of the later trade mark.

6. Any Member State may provide that, by derogation from paragraphs 1 to 5, the grounds for refusal of registration or invalidity in force in that State prior to the date on which the provisions necessary to comply with this Directive enter into force, shall apply to trade marks for which application has been made prior to that date.

Article 5   A1A–07

Rights conferred by a trade mark

1. The registered trade mark shall confer on the proprietor exclusive rights therein. The proprietor shall be entitled to prevent all third parties not having his consent from using in the course of trade:

(a) any sign which is identical with the trade mark in relation to goods or services which are identical with those for which the trade mark is registered;

(b) any sign where, because of its identity with, or similarity to, the trade mark and the identity or similarity of the goods or services covered by the trade mark and the sign, there exists a likelihood of confusion on the part of the public, which includes the likelihood of association between the sign and the trade mark.

2. Any Member State may also provide that the proprietor shall be entitled to prevent all third parties not having his consent from using in the course of trade any sign which is identical with, or similar to, the trade mark in relation to goods or services which are not similar to those for which the trade mark is registered, where the latter has a reputation in the Member State and where use of that sign without due cause takes unfair advantage of, or is detrimental to, the distinctive character or the repute of the trade mark.

3. The following, *inter alia*, may be prohibited under paragraphs 1 and 2:

(a) affixing the sign to the goods or to the packaging thereof;

(b) offering the goods, or putting them on the market or stocking them for these purposes under that sign, or offering or supplying services thereunder;

(c) importing or exporting the goods under the sign;

(d) using the sign on business papers and in advertising.

4. Where, under the law of the Member State, the use of a sign under the conditions referred to in 1(b) or 2 could not be prohibited before the date on which the provisions necessary to comply with this Directive entered into force in the Member State concerned, the rights conferred by the trade mark may not be relied on to prevent the continued use of the sign.

5. Paragraphs 1 to 4 shall not affect provisions in any Member State relating to the protection against the use of a sign other than for the purposes of distinguishing goods or services, where use of that sign without due cause takes unfair advantage of, or is detrimental to, the distinctive character or the repute of the trade mark.

A1A–08

Article 6

Limitation of the effects of a trade mark

1. The trade mark shall not entitle the proprietor to prohibit a third party from using, in the course of trade,
    (a) his own name or address;
    (b) indications concerning the kind, quality, quantity, intended purpose, value, geographical origin, the time of production of goods or of rendering of the service, or other characteristics of goods or services;
    (c) the trade mark where it is necessary to indicate the intended purpose of a product or service, in particular as accessories or spare parts;
provided he uses them in accordance with honest practices in industrial or commercial matters.
2. The trade mark shall not entitle the proprietor to prohibit a third party from using, in the course of trade, an earlier right which only applies in a particular locality if that right is recognized by the laws of the Member State in question and within the limits of the territory in which it is recognized.

A1A–09

Article 7

Exhaustion of the rights conferred by a trade mark

1. The trade mark shall not entitle the proprietor to prohibit its use in relation to goods which have been put on the market in the Community under that trade mark by the proprietor or with his consent.
2. Paragraph 1 shall not apply where there exist legitimate reasons for the proprietor to oppose further commercialization of the goods, especially where the condition of the goods is changed or impaired after they have been put on the market.

A1A–10

Article 8

Licensing

1. A trade mark may be licensed for some or all of the goods or services for which it is registered and for the whole or part of the Member State concerned. A license may be exclusive or non-exclusive.
2. The proprietor of a trade mark may invoke the rights conferred by that trade mark against a licensee who contravenes any provision in his licensing contract with regard to its duration, the form covered by the registration in which the trade mark may be used, the scope of the goods or services for which the licence is granted, the territory in which the trade mark may be affixed, or the quality of the goods manufactured or of the services provided by the licensee.

A1A–11

Article 9

Limitation in consequence of acquiescence

1. Where, in a Member State, the proprietor of an earlier trade mark as referred to in Article 4(2) has acquiesced, for a period of five successive years, in the use of a later trade mark registered in that Member State while being aware of such use, he shall no longer be entitled on the basis of the earlier trade mark either to apply for a declaration that the later trade mark is invalid or to oppose the use of the later trade

mark in respect of the goods or services for which the later trade mark has been used, unless registration of the later trade mark was applied for in bad faith.

2.   Any Member State may provide that paragraph 1 shall apply *mutatis mutandis* to the proprietor of an earlier trade mark referred to in Article 4(4)(a) or an other earlier right referred to in Article 4(4)(b) or (c).

3.   In the cases referred to in paragraphs 1 and 2, the proprietor of a later registered trade mark shall not be entitled to oppose the use of the earlier right, even though that right may no longer be invoked against the later trade mark.

Article 10   A1A–12

Use of trade marks

1.   If, within a period of five years following the date of the completion of the registration procedure, the proprietor has not put the trade mark to genuine use in the Member State in connection with the goods or services in respect of which it is registered, or if such use has been suspended during an uninterrupted period of five years, the trade mark shall be subject to the sanctions provided for in this Directive, unless there are proper reasons for non-use.

2.   The following shall also constitute use within the meaning of paragraph 1:
   (a) use of the trade mark in a form differing in elements which do not alter the distinctive character of the mark in the form in which it was registered;
   (b) affixing of the trade mark to goods or to the packaging thereof in the Member State concerned solely for export purposes.

3.   Use of the trade mark with the consent of the proprietor or by any person who has authority to use a collective mark or a guarantee or certification mark shall be deemed to constitute use by the proprietor.

4.   In relation to trade marks registered before the date on which the provisions necessary to comply with this Directive enter into force in the Member State concerned:
   (a) where a provision in force prior to that date attaches sanctions to non-use of a trade mark during an uninterrupted period, the relevant period of five years mentioned in paragraph 1 shall be deemed to have begun to run at the same time as any period of non-use which is already running at that date;
   (b) where there is no use provision in force prior to that date, the periods of five years mentioned in paragraph 1 shall be deemed to run from that date at the earliest.

Article 11   A1A–13

Sanctions for non use of a trade mark in legal or administrative proceedings

1.   A trade mark may not be declared invalid on the ground that there is an earlier conflicting trade mark if the latter does not fulfil the requirements of use set out in Article 10(1), (2) and (3) or in Article 10(4), as the case may be.

2.   Any Member State may provide that registration of a trade mark may not be refused on the ground that there is an earlier conflicting trade mark if the latter does not fulfil the requirements of use set out in Article 10(1), (2) and (3) or in Article 10(4), as the case may be.

3.   Without prejudice to the application of Article 12; where a counter-claim for revocation is made, any Member State may provide that a trade mark may not be successfully invoked in infringement proceedings if it is established as a result of a plea that the trade mark could be revoked pursuant to Article 12(1).

4.   If the earlier trade mark has been used in relation to part only of the goods or services for which it is registered, it shall, for purposes of applying paragraphs 1, 2 and 3, be deemed to be registered in respect only of that part of the goods or services.

A1A–14   *Article 12*

Grounds for revocation

1.   A trade mark shall be liable to revocation if, within a continuous period of five years, it has not been put to genuine use in the Member State in connection with the goods or services in respect of which it is registered, and there are no proper reasons for non-use; however, no person may claim that the proprietor's rights in a trade mark should be revoked where, during the interval between expiry of the five-year period and filing of the application for revocation, genuine use of the trade mark has been started or resumed; the commencement or resumption of use within a period of three months preceding the filing of the application for revocation which began at the earliest on expiry of the continuous period of five years of non-use, shall, however, be disregarded where preparations for the commencement or resumption occur only after the proprietor becomes aware that the application for revocation may be filed.

2.   A trade mark shall also be liable to revocation if, after the date on which it was registered,

   (a) in consequence of acts or inactivity of the proprietor, it has become the common name in the trade for a product or service in respect of which it is registered;

   (b) in consequence of the use made of it by the proprietor of the trade mark or with his consent in respect of the goods or services for which it is registered, it is liable to mislead the public, particularly as to the nature, quality or geographical origin of those goods or services.

A1A–15   *Article 13*

Grounds for refusal or revocation or invalidity relating to only some of the goods or services

Where grounds for refusal of registration or for revocation or invalidity of a trade mark exist in respect of only some of the goods or services for which that trade mark has been applied for or registered, refusal of registration or revocation or invalidity shall cover those goods or services only.

A1A–16   *Article 14*

Establishment *a posteriori* of invalidity or revocation of a trade mark

Where the seniority of an earlier trade mark which has been surrendered or allowed to lapse, is claimed for a Community trade mark, the invalidity or revocation of the earlier trade mark may be established *a posteriori*.

Article 15   **A1A–17**

Special provisions in respect of collective marks, guarantee marks and certification marks

1.   Without prejudice to Article 4, Member States whose laws authorize the registration of collective marks or of guarantee or certification marks may provide that such marks shall not be registered, or shall be revoked or declared invalid, on grounds additional to those specified in Articles 3 and 12 where the function of those marks so requires.

2.   By way of derogation from Article 3(1)(c), Member States may provide that signs or indications which may serve, in trade, to designate the geographical origin of the goods or services may constitute collective, guarantee or certification marks. Such a mark does not entitle the proprietor to prohibit a third party from using in the course of trade such signs or indications, provided he uses them in accordance with honest practices in industrial or commercial matters; in particular, such a mark may not be invoked against a third party who is entitled to use a geographical name.

Article 16   **A1A–18**

National provisions to be adopted pursuant to this Directive

1.   The Member States shall bring into force the laws, regulations and administrative provisions necessary to comply with this Directive not later than December 28, 1991. They shall immediately inform the Commission thereof.

2.   Acting on a proposal from the Commission, the Council, acting by qualified majority, may defer the date referred to in paragraph 1 until December 31, 1992, at the latest.

3.   Member States shall communicate to the Commission the text of the main provisions of national law which they adopt in the field governed by this Directive.

Article 17

Addressees   **A1A–19**

This Directive is addressed to the Member States.

Appendix 2

THE TRADE MARKS AND SERVICE MARKS RULES 1986

General points of procedure

Signature of documents   **A2–10**

Paragraph (2) of Rule 10 has been deleted, with effect from July 15, 1991, by S.I. 1991 No. 1431.

A2–14   Agents

Paragraph (5) of Rule 14 has been replaced, with effect from October 1, 1990, by the following (S.I. 1990 No. 1459):

"(5) The Registrar may refuse to recognise as agent in respect of any business under the 1938 Act or the modified 1938 Act—

(a) a person who has been convicted of an offence under section 283 of the Copyright, Designs and Patents Act 1988;

(b) an individual whose name has been erased from and not restored to the register of trade mark agents required to be kept pursuant to rules made under section 282 of the Copyright, Designs and Patents Act 1988 on the ground of misconduct;

(c) a person who is found by the Secretary of State to have been guilty of such conduct as would, in the case of an individual registered in that register, render him liable to have his name erased from it on the ground of misconduct;

(d) a partnership or body corporate of which one of the partners or directors is a person whom the Registrar could refuse to recognise under paragraph (a), (b) or (c) above".

Application for Registration

A2–21   Form of application for registration and request for amendment

In paragraph (1) of Rule 21, the words from "but if the applicant is a firm" to the end of the paragraph have been deleted, with effect from July 15, 1991 (S.I. 1991 No. 1431).

In paragraphs (2) and (3) of Rule 21, the reference to "form TM2" has been replaced by a reference to "Form TM3", with effect from October 1, 1990 (S.I. 1990 No. 1799).

Registration and Renewal

A2–59   Non-completion

Paragraph (8) of Rule 59 has been replaced, with effect from October 1, 1990, by the following (S.I. 1990 No. 1799):

"(8) For the purpose of this Rule, the requirements for completion are satisfied—

(a) in the case of an application made before 1st October 1990, when the Registrar has received the prescribed fee referred to in Rule 60(1) below and form TM10 duly completed; and

(b) in the case of an application made on or after 1st October 1990, when the Registrar has received form TM10A duly completed."

A2–60   Entry in Register

In paragraph (1) of Rule 60, the words from "and upon receipt of form TM10" to the end of the paragraph have been deleted and the following substituted:

"enter the mark in the register—

(a) in the case of an application made before 1st October 1990, upon receipt of form TM10, accompanied by the prescribed registration fee; and

(b) in the case of an application made on or after 1st October 1990, upon receipt of form TM10A."

Paragraph (2) of Rule 60 has been deleted. Both amendments were made by S.I. 1990 No. 1799 with effect from October 1, 1990.

Assignments and Transmissions

Particulars to be stated and copies of documents A2–73

Paragraph (2) of Rule 73 has been deleted, with effect from July 15, 1991 (S.I. 1991 No. 1431).

Entry of assignment or transmission in register A2–77

In paragraph (a) of Rule 77, all the words in brackets have been deleted, with effect from July 15, 1991 (S.I. 1991 No. 1431).

Registered Users

Application for entry of registered user A2–107

The words after "form TM50" in Rule 107 have been deleted, with effect from July 15, 1991 (S.I. 1991 No. 1431).

Entry of Registered User A2–108

In paragraph (2) of Rule 108, the words in brackets have been deleted, with effect from July 15, 1991 (S.I. 1991 No. 1431).

Calculation of times or periods A2–115

For paragraph (1) of Rule 115 the following has been substituted, with effect from August 1, 1989 (S.I. 1989 No. 1117):

"(1) Where, on any day, there is—

   (a) a general interruption or subsequent dislocation in the postal services of the United Kingdom, or

   (b) an event or circumstance causing an interruption in the normal operation of the Office,

the Registrar may certify the day as being one on which there is an "interruption" and, where any period of time specified in these Rules for the sending or filing of any notice, application or other document expires on a day so certified the period shall be extended to the first day next following (not being an excluded day) which is not so certified.

   (1A) Any certificate of the Registrar given pursuant to this rule shall be posted in the Office."

In paragraph (3) of Rule 115, the words "the interruption" have been substituted for the words "the period of interruption or dislocation", with effect from August 1, 1989 (S.I. 1989 No. 1117).

At the end of Rule 115, a new paragraph (4) has been inserted as follows, with effect from August 1, 1989 (S.I. 1989 No. 1117):

"(4) If in any particular case the Registrar is satisfied that the failure to file any notice, application or other document within any period of time specified in these Rules or within the period of six months specified in section 39A(1) of the 1938 Act or of the modified 1938 Act was wholly or mainly attributable to a failure or undue delay in the postal services in the United Kingdom, the Registrar may, if he thinks fit, extend the period of time so that it ends on the day of the receipt by the addressee of the notice, application or other document (or, if the day of such receipt is an excluded day, on the first following day which is not an excluded day), or, in the case of the said period of six months, determine that the application shall be treated as having been made within that period, in each case upon such notice to other parties and upon such terms as he may direct."

TRADE MARK FORMS

Form TM2 has been replaced by Form TM3 (below), with effect from October 1, 1990 (S.I. 1990 No. 1801).   **A2–502**

The Patent Office

Trade Marks
Form TM3

Application for Registration
of a Trade or Service Mark

		For official use
1.	If this application is part of a companion group enter in the box the total number of applications within the group (including this one).	
2.	The application will be examined for registrability in Part A unless "B" is entered in the box.	
3.	Indicate type of mark *(tick **one** box)* Device only: Word only: Device and word: Stylised word:	
4.	Enter class number to which this application relates.	
5.	Particular requirements relating to this mark or specification. Enter here limitations, for example disclaimers or translations.	

	For official use
6. If this application relates to a series of marks enter the total number in the series.	

7. If this application is connected with a registered user application, tick relevant box.
   If you are applying under Section 29(1)(b) of the Trade Marks Act a form TM50 must accompany the application.

   Section 28:

   Section 29(1)(b):

   If this application is being made under Section 29(1)(a) of the Act, tick this box.

8. If this application is to be considered under International Convention / priority enter country and date claimed.

   Country:

   Date:

9. Representation of mark(s) applied for

THE TRADE MARKS AND SERVICE MARKS RULES 1986

	For official use
10. Applicant details Applicant's Patent Office ADP number *(if known)*: _____ Name: _____ Address: _____ _____ County/ Postcode/ State: _____ Zipcode: _____ Country: _____	
11. Enter Country of Incorporation and if appropriate State of Incorporation. Country: _____ State: _____	
12. Agent's details Agent's Patent Office ADP number: _____ Name: _____ Address: _____ _____ County: _____ Postcode: _____ Telephone STD Telephone contact: _____ code: _____ number: _____	
Agent's own reference _____	
13. Address for service ADP number *(if known)*: _____ Name: _____ Address: _____ _____ County: _____ Postcode: _____	

14. Enter here the specification of goods or services to which this application relates.	For official use

To be completed by person or firm completing the form.

Signature:

Name
(BLOCK letters):

Telephone number for contact
purposes (if not entered in Section 12):   Date:

Check list
When you have filled in the form, tick the boxes below to show you have:

Enclosed the necessary fee ☐

Enclosed a copy of form TM50 if
applying for registration of registered
user under Section 29(1)(b) of the
Trade Marks Act 1938 ☐

Enclosed 4 copies of a
representation of the mark each
on a separate form TM4 ☐

Enclosed any continuation
sheets (if appropriate) ☐

A new form TM10, below, has replaced the old version, with effect from **A2–510** October 1, 1990 (S.I. 1990 No. 1801).

The Patent Office

Trade Marks
Form TM10

Payment of Registration fee
for a Trade or Service Mark

1. Trade or Service Mark application number:

    Class number:

2. Number of the journal in which this application was advertised:

3. Address for service:

    Patent Office ADP number *(if known)*:

    Name:

    Address:

    Postcode:

    Telephone contact: STD code: Telephone number:

4. **Declaration**

    I/We declare that any written undertakings given to the Registrar to send notice of the advertisement of the application to other proprietors have been fulfilled. To the best of my/our knowledge and belief, either the period or extended period for filing opposition to the application has expired without any notice of opposition having been filed, or any oppositions filed have finally been determined in favour of the applicant.

    Applicant's name:

    Signature: Date: 19

    Status:

    Checklist

    When you have filled in the form, tick the boxes below to show you have:

    Fulfilled all the written undertakings described in the declaration at box 4

    Enclosed the necessary fee   Signed at box 4

A2–510A   A new form TM10A, below – Completion of Registration of a Trade or Service Mark – has been introduced, with effect from October 1, 1990 (S.I. 1990 No. 1801).

The Patent Office

Trade Marks
Form TM10A

Completion of Registration
of a Trade or Service Mark

❑ *There is no fee for filing this form*

1. Trade or Service Mark application number:

   Class number:

2. Number of the journal in which this
   application was advertised:

3. Address for service:

   Patent Office ADP
   number *(if known)*:

   Name:

   Address:

   Postcode:

   Telephone
   contact: STD
                         code: Telephone
                                        number:

4. **Declaration**

   I/We declare that any written undertakings given to the Registrar to send notice
   of the advertisement of the application to other proprietors have been fulfilled.
   To the best of my/our knowledge and belief, either the period or extended
   period for filing opposition to the application has expired without any notice of
   opposition having been filed, or any oppositions filed have finally been
   determined in favour of the applicant.

   Applicant's name:

   Signature: Date: 19

   Status:

   Checklist

   When you have filled in the form, tick the boxes below to show you have:

   Fulfilled all the written undertakings
   described in the declaration at box 4   Signed at box 4

A new form TM11, below, has replaced the old version, with effect from **A2–511** October 1, 1990 (S.I. 1990 No. 1801).

The Patent Office

Trade Marks
Form TM11

Form for renewal
of Registration

1. Name of proprietor as
   entered on the register:

2. Name and address of agent
   or address for service:

   Telephone   STD   Telephone
   contact: _____ code: _____ number: _____

                   ADP   Your
   Date: _____ no: _____ ref: _____

3. Payment of renewal fee

Due date of renewal	Registration number	Class	Advertised in Trade Marks Journal number *(if available)*	Fee

4. Name and address of person paying the fee *(if not the registered proprietor)*

   Name: _____

   Address: _____

   _____

   _____ Postcode: _____

Declaration

I declare that I am directed by the proprietor of the above
numbered mark to pay the requested Renewal Fee.

Signature: _____ Date: _____

Additional fee (late payment):

*Please send this form and your fee to the address
shown in the enclosed explanatory notes.*

A2–600 NOTE: The fees change almost every year. The current fees rules are as follows:

The Trade Marks and Service Marks (Fees) Rules 1992

(as amended by S.I. 1993 No. 3029)

Made - - - -	*29th April 1992*
Laid before Parliament	*30th April 1992*
Coming into force	*11th May 1992*

Whereas in pursuance of the requirements of section 40(3) of the Trade Marks Act 1938, the Secretary of State has, before making the following Rules under that Act, published notice of his intention to make such Rules and of the place where copies of the draft Rules might be obtained by advertising such notice in the Trade Marks Journal and the Official Journal (Patents) on 11th March 1992 and 18th March 1992, being the manner in which he considered most expedient so as to enable persons affected to make representations to him before the Rules were finally settled:

Now, therefore, the Secretary of State, in exercise of the powers conferred by sections 40, 41 and 68(1) of the Trade Marks Act 1938 and now vested in him, of the power conferred on him by the Department of Trade and Industry (Fees) Order 1988, and of all other powers enabling him in that behalf, after consultation with the Council on Tribunals pursuant to section 10(1) of the Tribunals and Inquiries Act 1971 and with the sanction of the Treasury pursuant to the said section 41, hereby makes the following Rules:—

1.—(1) These Rules may be cited as the Trade Marks and Service Marks (Fees) Rules 1992 and shall come into force on 11th May 1992.

(2) The Trade Marks and Service Marks (Fees) Rules 1991 are hereby revoked.

2. These Rules shall be construed as one with the Trade Marks and Service Marks Rules 1986.

3. The fees to be paid in respect of any matters arising under the Trade Marks Act 1938 shall be those specified in the Schedule to these Rules; and in any case where a form specified in the Schedule as the corresponding form in relation to any matter is required by the Trade Marks and Service Marks Rules 1986 to be used, that form shall be accompanied by the fee, if any, specified in respect of that matter.

T. Sainsbury
Minister for Industry,
23rd April 1992   Department of Trade and Industry

We sanction the making of these Rules.

I. Patnick
N. Baker
Two of the Lords Commissioners
29th April 1992   of Her Majesty's Treasury

The Trade Marks and Service Marks (Fees) Rules 1992

SCHEDULE

Rule 3

FEES PAYABLE

(In this Schedule, references to a section or a Schedule are references to that section of or Schedule to the Trade Marks Act 1938 as it has effect with respect to trade marks or with respect to service marks, as the context may require; and references to a rule are references to that rule of the Trade Marks and Service Marks Rules 1986.)

Number of corresponding form	Item	Amount £
TM3	On application to register a trade mark, a service mark or a series of trade marks or service marks for a specification of goods or services included in one class, (whether or not accepted for registration)—	185
TM5	On request to the Registrar to state grounds of decision relating to an application to register a trade mark or a service mark and materials used—	100
TM6	On application to register a certification trade mark for a specification of goods included in one class, or in respect of each class on application made at the same time to register one certification trade mark for specifications of goods not all included in one class, (whether or not accepted for registration)—	185
TM7	On notice of opposition before the Registrar under section 18 or paragraph 2(2) of Schedule 1, for each application opposed, by opponent—	—
TM8	On filing a counterstatement in answer to a notice of opposition under section 18 or paragraph 2(2) of Schedule 1, for each application opposed, by the applicant; or in answer to an application under section 26, 27, 32 or 33 by the proprietor in respect of each trade mark or service mark; or in answer to a notice of opposition under section 35 or 36, for each application or conversion opposed, by the proprietor—	—
TM10	In respect of an application to register filed before 1st October 1990, for registration of a trade mark (including a certification or defensive trade mark), a service mark or a series of trade marks or service marks for a specification of goods or services included in one class; or in respect of each class for registration upon applications made at the same time of one certification trade mark for specifications of goods not all included in one class—	115

SCHEDULE (*continued*)

Number of correspon- ding form	Item	Amount £
TM11	For renewal of registration of a trade mark, a service mark or a series of trade marks or service marks at expiration of last registration; or in respect of each class for renewal of registrations of the same certification trade mark with the same date for goods in more than one class—	275
TM11	Additional fee under rule 67—	30
TM13	Restoration fee under Rule 68—	100
TM16	On application to register a subsequent proprietor in a case of assignment or transmission of one or more trade marks or service marks—	50
TM19	On application to disolve the association between registered trade marks, registered service marks or both registered trade marks and registered service marks—	—
TM23	For striking out goods or services from those for which a trade mark or a service mark is registered on the request of the registered proprietor—	30
TM24	On request by registered proprietor of a trade mark or a service mark for entry of disclaimer or memorandum in the register—	30
TM25	On application to the Registrar for leave to add to or alter a registered trade mark or service mark—	30
TM26	On application under section 26, 27, 32 or 33 for rectification of the register or removal of a trade mark or a service mark from the register—	—
TM27	On application for leave to intervene in proceedings under section 26, 27, 32 or 33 for rectification of the register or removal of a trade mark or a service mark from the register—	—
TM30	On appeal from the Registrar, otherwise than to the Court, in respect of each decision appealed against, by appellant—	—
TM31	For certificate of the Registrar (other than certification under section 19(2)) of the registration of a trade mark, a service mark or a series of trade marks or service marks—	20

SCHEDULE (*continued*)

Number of correspon-ding form	Item	Amount £
TM32	On application to register a defensive trade mark for a specification of goods included in one class, (whether or not accepted for registration)—	185
TM35	On request by the registered proprietor of a certification trade mark to permit alteration of the deposited regulations thereof:	
	for the regulations of one such registration—	—
	and for the same or substantially the same regulations of each other registration proposed to be altered in the same way and included in the same request—	—
TM36	On application under Rule 93 to expunge or vary the registration of a certification trade mark or to vary the deposited regulations of a certification trade mark or of certification trade marks of the same registered proprietor where the regulations are substantially the same—	—
TM37	On notice to the Secretary of State of opposition under paragraph 2(2) of Schedule 1, for each application opposed, by the opponent—	—
TM40	On application for certificate of the Registrar under section 22(5) or approval of the Registrar under section 22(6):	
	for the first mark proposed to be assigned or transmitted—	—
	and for every other mark included in the same assignment or transmission—	—
TM43	On application for directions by the Registrar for advertisement of assignment of trade marks or service marks in use, without goodwill:	
	for the first mark assigned—	—
	and for every other mark assigned with the same devolution or title—	—
TM45[1]	On application by registered proprietor under Rule 6 for conversion of specification—	—

[1] The fee of £20 payable upon application for conversion was abolished with effect from December 29, 1993 (S.I. 1993 No. 3029).

SCHEDULE (*continued*)

Number of correspon- ding form	Item	Amount £
TM46	On notice of opposition to a conversion of the specification or specifications of a registered trade mark or registered trade marks: for the first mark— and for every other mark of the same proprietor having the same specification—	— —
TM47	On notice of opposition to application for leave to add to or alter registered trade marks or service marks, for each application opposed—	—
TM48	For every entry in the register of a rectification thereof or an alteration therein ordered by the Court—	—
TM49	On request to enter in the register and advertise a certificate of validity under section 47: for the first registration certified— and for every other registration certified in the same certificate—	— —
TM50	On application to register a registered user of a registered trade mark or a registered service mark in respect of goods or services within the specification thereof—	30
TM51	On application by the proprietor of a single trade mark or a single service mark under section 28(8)(a) to vary entry of a registered user thereof—	—
TM51	On application by the proprietor of more than one trade mark or service mark under section 28(8)(a) to vary the entries of a registered user thereof: for the first mark— and for every other mark of the proprietor for which the same user is registered included in the application—	— —
TM54	On notice under section 28(9) of the intention to intervene in one proceeding for the variation or cancellation of entries of a registered user of trade marks or service marks—	—
TM55	For the continuance of a cotton mark in each class of the collection of refused marks at the end of each period of fourteen years after the date of the application—	100

SCHEDULE (*continued*)

Number of correspon- ding form	Item	Amount £
TM56	For certificate of the Keeper of an entry in the Manchester Record relating to one trade mark or a series of trade marks—	20
—	On request for the Registrar's preliminary advice under Rule 20, for each trade mark or service mark submitted in respect of one class at the same time:	
	for the first mark—	35
	and for each additional mark—	12
—	For certifying office copies, manuscripts or photographic or printed matter, each—	20
—	For inspecting register or Manchester Record, or notice of opposition, counterstatement or decision in connection with any rectification of the register relating to any particular trade mark or service mark—	1

The fee to be paid on any proceedings at the Manchester Branch and at the office of the Cutlers' Company shall be the same as for the similar proceeding at the Office.

For the purpose of these fees (except as specifically provided above) every mark of a series under section 21, or any preceding similar enactment, shall be deemd to be a mark separately registered.

RULES OF THE SUPREME COURT

ORDER 100

A5–02   *Appeals and applications under the Trade Marks Act 1938*

New Sub-rules 2(7) and 2(8) have been added to Order 100 by R.S.C. (Amendment No. 3) 1989 (S.I. 1989 No. 1307), with effect from September 1, 1989: 2(7) Where an application is made under section 58C of the Trade Marks Act 1938 the applicant shall serve notice of the application on all persons so far as reasonably ascertainable having an interest in the goods or material which are the subject of the application, including any person in whose favour an order could be made in respect of the goods or material under the said section of the Act of 1938 or under section 114, 204 or 231 of the Copyright, Designs and Patents Act 1988.

2(8) An application under the said section 58C shall be made by originating summons or, if it is made in a pending action, by summons or motion in that action.

APPENDIX 11

Patents, Designs and Marks Act 1986

SCHEDULE 2

PART I

REFERENCES TO TRADE MARKS TO INCLUDE REFERENCES TO SERVICE MARKS

A11–06   The following have been deleted from Schedule 2 by section 303(2) and Schedule 8 of the Copyright, Designs and Patents Act 1988, with effect from August 1, 1989:
— the whole of paragraph 1(2)(a).
— the words "subsection (1)(j) of section 396 and" in paragraph 1(2)(k).
— the words "subsection 2(i) of section 93" in paragraph 1(2)(l).

APPENDIX 12

THE PARIS CONVENTION

A12–47   **Convention Countries**

The Convention countries are listed in the Trade Marks and Service Marks (Relevant Countries) Order (S.I. 1986 No. 1303). This statutory instrument is amended from time to time by other S.I.s which have made the following changes:

— the inclusion of Belarus, Croatia, The Czech Republic, Kazakhstan, the Slovak Republic, Slovenia, the Russian Federation and the Ukraine;
— the removal of the reference to Czechoslovakia;
— the substitution of Germany for both the German Democratic Republic (and Berlin (East)) and Germany, Federal Republic of (and Berlin (West)).

The list at the time of writing is as follows:

RELEVANT COUNTRIES FOR TRADE MARKS

Algeria
Argentina
Australia (including Norfolk Island)
Austria
Bahamas
Barbados
Belarus
Belgium
Benin
Brazil
Bulgaria
Burkina
Burundi
Cameroon
Canada
Central African Republic
Chad
China, People's Republic of
Congo, People's Republic of
Côte d'Ivoire
Croatia
Cuba
Cyprus, Republic of
Czech
Denmark (including the Faroe Islands)
Dominican Republic
Ecuador
Egypt
Finland
France (including all Overseas Departments and Territories)
Gabon
Germany
Ghana
Greece
Guinea, Republic of
Haiti
Holy See
Honduras
Hong Kong
Hungary
Iceland

Indonesia
Iran
Iraq
Ireland, Republic of
Israel
Italy
Japan
Jordan
Kazakhstan
Kenya
Korea, Republic of
Lebanon
Libya
Liechtenstein
Luxembourg
Madagascar
Malagasy Republic
Malawi
Mali
Malta
Mauritania
Mauritius
Mexico
Monaco
Mongolian People's Republic
Morocco
Netherlands (including Aruba and the Netherlands Antilles)
New Zealand
Niger
Nigeria
Norway
Philippines
Poland
Portugal
Romania
Russian Federation
Rwanda
San Marino
Senegal
Slovak Republic
Slovenia
South Africa
Soviet Union
Spain
Sri Lanka
Sudan
Suriname
Sweden
Switzerland
Syria
Tanzania
Togo

Trinidad and Tobago
Tunisia
Turkey
Uganda
Ukraine
United States of America (including Puerto Rico and all territories and possessions)
Uruguay
Vietnam
Yugoslavia
Zaire
Zambia
Zimbabwe

APPENDIX 13

LIST OF CONTRASTED MARKS AND NAMES

(2) *Contrasted words*

"Bensyl" too close to "Bentasil" and "Benvil": *"Bensyl"* [1992] R.P.C. 529 **A13–03**
(B.o.T.).

"Inadine" too close to "Anadin": *"Inadine"* [1992] R.P.C. 421.

"Lancer" allowed notwithstanding "Lancia": *"Lancer"* [1987] R.P.C. 303 (C.A.).

"Portoblast" an infringement of "Porta": *Portakabin v. Powerblast* [1990] R.P.C. 471.

"Primasport" allowed notwithstanding "Primark": *"Primasport"* [1992] F.S.R. 515.

"Star" too close to "Spar": *"Star"* [1990] R.P.C. 522 (Regy.).

"Terbuline" too close to "Terbolan" and "Terbalin": *"Terbuline"* [1990] R.P.C. 21 (B.o.T.).

"Torre Nova" allowed notwithstanding "Torres": *"Torre Nova"* [1991] R.P.C. 109.

"Thermos Prima" allowed notwithstanding "Primark": *"Thermos Prima"* [1991] R.P.C. 120.

"Treat Size" would neither deceive nor confuse in the light of "Treats": *Mars G.B. v. Cadbury* [1987] R.P.C. 387.

"Univer" too close to "Univet": *"Univer"* [1993] R.P.C. 239.

INDEX